GROWING STRONG IN THE SEASONS OF LIFE:

SPRING

GROWING STRONG IN THE SEASONS OF LIFE: SPRING

CHARLES R. SWINDOLL

FOREWORD BY
BILLY GRAHAM

WALKER AND COMPANY · NEW YORK

Large Print Edition by arrangement with Multnomah Press

First Large Print Edition published in the United States of America in 1989
by Walker Publishing Company, Inc.

Published simultaneously in Canada by Thomas Allen & Son Canada, Limited, Markham, Ontario

Library of Congress Cataloging-in-Publication Data
Swindoll, Charles R.
Growing strong in the seasons of life. Spring / Charles R. Swindoll ; foreword by Billy Graham.—1st large print ed.
p. cm.
Originally published in 1 vol.: Growing strong in the seasons of life. Portland, Or. : Multnomah Press, c1983.
Bibliography: p.
ISBN 0-8027-2635-6 (lg. print)
1. Devotional exercises. 2. Spring—Religious aspects—Christianity. 3. Large type books. I. Title.
[BV4832.2.S8853 1989]
242′.2—dc20 89-34705
CIP

Printed in the United States of America
10 8 6 4 2 1 3 5 7 9

With gratitude and delight I dedicate this volume to
EDGAR AND CANDEE NEUENSCHWANDER
who have been loving and supportive during the
cold winters, the changing springs, the hot
summers and the busy autumns of the
past twelve years of my life.
Through it all they have proven themselves faithful
friends both in season and out of season.

CONTENTS

FOREWORD

On various occasions popular musical artists will release special albums that represent their best efforts. The titles are familiar to all of us: "The Best of Sinatra" . . . "The Best of Streisand" . . . "The best of Neil Diamond." It is not uncommon for these albums to push their way quickly to the top of the hit parade as music lovers listen again and again to their favorite artists doing their best work.

This volume by your friend and mine could be called "The Best of Charles Swindoll." For almost ten years this man has ministered to our world through books, several of which have become (and still are) bestsellers. All of us have come to expect high quality and unusual insights as we pick up another book to which he has put his pen . . . and we have not once been disappointed.

Here is another winner. *Growing Strong in the Seasons of Life* is not only a beautiful statement about four distinct "seasons," it is also a healthy and balanced diet of hope for the discouraged, a refuge for the hurting, a challenge for the weary, and a friend for the lonely. You will smile with understanding and you may even weep with compassion. You will appreciate how carefully Scripture is woven into the fabric of each page, sometimes boldly, but more often softly, artistically.

May you find the living Lord opening His arms of love to you as you move through each of these four seasons. Take your time. Walk slowly. Feel God's presence as you consider the days and weeks and years that He has given to you. Ask Him to bring new strength to your soul.

With delight I recommend "The Best of Charles Swindoll" to you. Here is a combination of words, phrases, and ideas you'll want to read again and again. A book for all seasons.

Billy Graham

INTRODUCTION

I am glad God changes the times and the seasons, aren't you?

Just think how dull things would become if He didn't paint nature's scenes in different colors several times a year. With infinite creativity and remarkable regularity, He splashes white over brown and orange over green, giving such attention to detail that we are often stunned with amazement.

Each of the four seasons offers fresh and vital insights for those who take the time to look and to think. Hidden beneath the surface are colorful yet silent truths that touch most every area across the landscape of our lives. As each three-month segment of every year holds its own mysteries and plays its own melodies, offering sights and smells, feelings and fantasies altogether distinct, so it is in the seasons of life. The Master is neither mute nor careless as He alters our times and changes our seasons. How wrong to trudge blindly and routinely through a lifetime of changing seasons without discovering answers to the new mysteries and learning to sing the new melodies! Seasons are designed to deepen us, to instruct us in the wisdom and ways of our God. To help us grow strong . . . like a tree planted by the rivers of water.

This is a book about one of the seasons: autumn. It offers a series of suggestions and ideas to help you read

God's signals with a sensitive heart. Quietly and deliberately, we'll walk together through each scene, pondering the subtle shading as well as the obvious broad brush strokes from the Artist's hand. Let's take our time and leave room for our feelings to emerge. Let's sing inharmony with the Composer's music. Let's drink in the beauty of His handiwork. It will take time, so let's not hurry.

Our hope is to grow stronger and taller as our roots dig deeper in the soft soil along the banks of the river of life. And let's not fear the winds of adversity! The gnarled old twisted trees, beaten and buffeted by wind and weather along the ocean shores, tell their own stories of consistent courage. May God make us strong as the winds whip against us, my friend. Roots grow deep when the winds are strong. Let's commit ourselves to growing strong in the seasons of life.

Just before we embark on our journey, allow me a final few paragraphs concerning the composition of these thoughts.

When my family and I moved to Fullerton in the summer of 1971, I immediately began writing a weekly column in our church newsletter, which I called "Think It Over." I have continued that discipline to this day. Little did I realize the far-reaching effect these provocative articles would some day have on our generation! I must express my gratitude to the staff of Multnomah Press for their creative sensitivity and bold vision to publish this material in various formats and titles since 1977. *For Those Who Hurt; Starting Over; Standing Out; Killing Giants, Pulling Thorns; Make Up Your*

Mind; and *Encourage Me* have emerged from the original "Think It Over" articles. We have all been amazed to see how broadly God has used and continues to use each one of those books in peoples' lives. I confess, *I have been the most surprised of all!* (I've been tempted to publish the letters from those who wrote me, describing how God used the books in their lives.) This volume is a compilation of several previously published articles that first appeared in those books, plus numerous other columns never before published. I am especially indebted to Julie Cave and Larry Libby for their loving friendshsip over the years. Because of their skilled insight and creative editorial assistance. I was able to see how such varied columns fit so beautifully into the theme of the seasons.

And once again, I declare my gratitude to Helen Peters, my personal secretary, for her unselfish patience with me, along with her relentless devotion to the task of typing and retyping the original manuscript.

Now . . . let's walk together as God escorts us through the seasons. Let's listen closely to His voice as we observe the changing scenery. It might be wise for us to brace ourselves against those strong gusts of wind that inevitably accompany each season. But even the storms beat a message of encouragement for us:

Deeper roots make for stronger lives.

Charles R. Swindoll

As I sit here in my home writing these words, it is the first day of spring. Literally. I'm ready for a new season, aren't you? Especially spring.

Colorful little pansy blooms are fluttering in the breeze alongside the winding brick walkway out front. I can see them through my study window. Two sparrows (I guess that's what they are) are playing fly 'n' seek. They are either madly in love or really ticked off at each other. They've built a tiny nest in the streetlight near the mailbox. Tiny pink buds now cover our ruby-leaf plum tree up near the window, and the grass is decidedly greener than it was a couple of months ago. God's private urban renewal program is happening before my very eyes in my yard. I was wrong again. Just when I was convinced everything was doomed to perpetual drab, it's become rainbow city out there. Amazing!

Reminds me of a slice of my life . . . how about you? The blizzard blast of winter does a numbing number on our minds, have you noticed? Feelings of helplessness settle in. The fragrance of blossoms seems buried forever, smothered beneath the cold, snuffed out in the root system . . . never again to emerge. Makes us wonder if we'll ever run free again, if the sod will ever soften, if we'll ever again feel warmly embraced by the rays of the sun as it smiles on us through cloudless days. Bottom line: Will change ever occur?

Suddenly, God pushes back the gate and in marches March to the cadence of the Conductor's command. Happens every year. Enter: renewal. exit: doubt. Hello hope, good-bye despair.

O Spring, how we've missed you!

How much we need your gracious nudging! Stir us from our slumber. Bring back the color. Add a little shower now and then to clean things up. Blow away those threatening clouds with your sweet, gentle breezes so we can see again the mountains of challenge that make us want to climb higher. They've been there all winter, but we've been inside a long, long time. It's easy to lose sight of the beautiful peaks and the lovely meadows when we reduce life to "Operation Survival."

Is it springtime right now in your season of life? Perhaps you're awakening from spiritual hibernation, crawling slowly out of a dark cave of disillusionment and discouragement. Don't be afraid to try again. That's the sun out there! It invites you to try out its splendor . . . to believe anew. To realize that the same Lord who renews the trees with buds and blossoms, who renews the grass with green in place of brown, is ready to renew your life with hope and courage (April 15, notwithstanding!).

The promise of change is all around. If you are ready to believe that, read on. The following "spring thoughts" have been designed with you in mind.

Roots

There's this tree in my front yard that gives me fits several times a year. It leans. No, it never breaks or stops growing . . . it just leans. It's attractive, deep green, nicely shaped, and annually bears fragrant blossoms. But let a good, healthy gust give it a shove—and over it goes. Like, *fast*.

It happened today. Right now the thing is tilted on about a forty-five degree angle towards the north. Stake and all, over it went. Seems such a shame this good-looking, charming tree can't hold its own. Take away the support ropes and it's only a matter of time . . . no match against the invisible slugger with a wild haymaker. Unless I lift it up, it will stay down for the full count. Every time.

Why? Well, in layman's language, it's top-heavy. Lots of leafy branches and heavy foliage above ground (which all of us appreciate and enjoy), but down underneath, weak roots. Little shoots here and there, reaching out for water and nutrients . . . but insufficient to support the fast-growing stuff up above. And the thing doesn't have sense enough to lay back on the new leaves until the roots catch up!

So out I go in the morning to bring it back up straight.

I'll talk to it, give it a piece of my mind I can't afford to lose, and with a jerk, tell it to "straighten up." But let another blustery bully come roarin' out of his corner and I'll guarantee you it will fall victim to a sucker punch before the third round.

If nothing else, that overgrown, ornery perennial has provided me with an object lesson I can't ignore any longer: Strong roots stabilize growth. If that's true of trees it is certainly crucial for Christians. Roots strengthen and support us against the prevailing winds of persuasion. When the mind-bending gales attack without warning, it's the network of solid roots that holds us firm and keeps us straight. Beautiful branches and lacy leaves, no matter how attractive, fail to fortify us as the velocity increases. It takes roots, stubborn, deep, powerful roots, to keep us standing.

that explains why the Savior said what He did about the plant that withered. It had a root problem (Mark 4:6), so it couldn't handle the blistering rays of the sun. And why Paul's prayer for those young, energetic Ephesian believers included the thought of "being rooted and grounded . . ." (3:17). And why the apostle urged the Colossian Christians to be "firmly rooted . . . built up and established" in their faith (2:7). Strong roots stabilize growth. That's the reason they are so very important. Without them we lean and sometimes snap.

But before you get excited about whipping up a strong set of roots, better remember this: It takes time. There's no instant route to roots. And it isn't fun 'n' games either. It's hard work. Nor is it a high-profile process. Nobody spends much time digging around a tree trunk, admiring: *"What neat roots you have!"* No, the stronger and deeper the roots, the less visible they are. The less noticed.

Mark it down—there won't be a seminar next week that promises "Strong roots in five days or your money back." The process is slow. Neither will there ever be a lot of noise and smoke surrounding their growth. The process is silent. But in the long run the final product will be irreplaceable . . . invaluable.

If you're looking for a showy, shallow, get-up-there-quick kind of growth, then I've got the answer. Drop by soon and I'll sell you a perfect specimen—ropes and all.

Cheap.

Deepening Your Roots
Mark 4:1-41; Ephesians 3:1-21; Colossians 2:1-23

Branching Out

1. Deepen your roots today by spending one solid hour reading Scripture. Then write down one key thought or promise that strengthened you out of that reading.
2. Buy a tree, plant it in your yard, and let it be a constant reminder of your need to grow deep roots.

Newborn

Two hours away from our own front door we traveled completely around the world. We didn't miss a continent. From Paraguay to the Congo. From the Serengeti Plains of Tanzania into the tropical rain forests of Malagasy, across the Indian Ocean to mysterious Malaya. Then it was the tundra of the Arctic Circle, Scandinavia to Mesopotamia, Egypt to China, Manchuria to Siberia. From the icy heights of the Himalayan peaks, across the vast outback of Australia, on deep into the tangled jungles of New Guinea. . . .

By bus.

In only forty-five minutes.

We *ooohd* and *ahhhd* our way through every conceivable scent, sight, and sound. Nothing was the same, except the small familiar sign that kept popping up on the trails and the trees: Please Don't Feed the Animals.

You guessed it. The famed San Diego Zoo earned another blue ribbon. Where else can a family hear the shrill scream of peacocks running free, touch an elephant's snout, study in detail the colorful crest of a rare cockatoo, look into the ceaseless stare of a silvery gray koala perched on the forked branches of a eucalyptus, or stand eighteen inches from a cobra . . . all in one afternoon? I'll tell you, it makes the child come out from inside us. As we marvel at God's handiwork among His creatures, we gain a renewed respect for His creative genius. Who else could ever come up with a fat-tailed *gecko*? Or the two-toned *tapir*? Or that weird, long-tongued *okapi* . . . part horseand part giraffe(!) . . . with fur like velvet and enormous ears?

Above and beyond all this, we had a rare treat seldom witnessed in that hundred-acre nucleus of Balboa Park. It was *so* unusual that our salty guide was suddenly mute. We happened upon a newborn. Can't remember the four-footed species, but the tiny thing was no more than two minutes old. There it lay out in the open. Still curled as though in the womb. Wet, wide-eyed, and flop-eared, that awkward, fuzzy ball of new life was blinking at its very first glimpse of dirt, rock, sun, and water. Standing over it was its mama, fresh blood on her strong hind legs as she proudly licked away the afterbirth and the cord. The other animals? Hardly a second glance. They milled around totally unconcerned.

We could stay no longer. We had to "stay on schedule," so we roared off, leaving a choking cloud of diesel exhaust in our wake.

Many moons have passed since that memorable episode, yet I can't get over the analogy. What happened down there is an amazingly accurate scenario of what happens every day around our world. Not physically, but spiritually. Not among caged animals, but in human hearts. Whether in Madagascar or Monterrey, Zaire or Zurich, Belfast or Birmingham, as traffic swirls by and the pace increases and pressure mounts . . . a new birth from heaven suddenly transpires. For some, it's in the heat of the day ánd for others it happens toward evening or in the dead of night. Some newborns take their first breath in a small church on a windswept hill after hearing the simple yet stirring story of the Savior's death. Others are in a lonely prison cell sitting beside a radio. Still others are on a campus surrounded by a few Christians who care.

God steps in. Unannounced, He bursts into the soul, bringing forgiveness, cleansing, peace, a whole new perspective and imension. He calls it "eternal life." And the newborn? Whether an ignorant savage in West Irian or an influential statesman on Capitol Hill, it really doesn't matter. The Scriptures paint the same portrait for all newborns:

> . . . a new creature . . . old things passed away . . . new things have come (2 Corinthians 5:17).

New hope. New attitudes. New feelings. New direction. New destiny. The newborn shakes its head, blinks, looks around at his first glimpse of new life,and he can hardly believe it. And the world? Why, of course, it rushes on. Unconcerned, busy, preoccupied; it has to "stay on schedule." Someone's eternal new birth has occurred. Although it doesn't attract a second glance from those standing around, God's kingdom is being silently enlarged.

It happens every day in our vast world. It even happened *today*. For all you know, maybe two minutes away from your own front door.

Deepening Your Roots
John 3:1-17; 2 Corinthians 5:17; 1 Peter 1:1-5

Branching Out
1. Sometime this week hold a baby in your arms.
2. Pray for a young Christian every day this week.

A Cure for Tunnel Vision

The splinter in my thumb this morning brings back pleasant memories of yesterday's diversion. Cranking up the old radial arm saw in my garage, I wound up with two pecky cedar window box planters. I plunged into the project with the zeal of a paratrooper, ecstatic over the airborne sawdust, delighting over every angle, every nail, every hammer blow, even the feel of the wood and the scream of the saw. I caught myself thinking about nothing but the next cut . . . the exhilaration of accomplishment . . . the sheer joy of doing something totally opposite of my career and completely different from my calling.

Periodically, I looked up through the sawdust and prayed, "Lord, I sure do like doing this!" In this terror-filled aspirin age, my saw and I gave each other wide, toothy grins.

It was Sir William Osler, the Canadian-born physician and distinguished professor of medicine at Johns Hopkins University, who once told an audience of medical men:

> No man is really happy or safe without a hobby, and it makes precious little difference what the outside interest may be—botany, beetles or butterflies; roses, tulips or

> irises; fishing, mountaineering or antiques—anything will do as long as he straddles a hobby and rides it hard.[1]

A worthier prescription was never penned. Diversions are essential to our health and personal development as schools are to our education, or as food is to our nourishment. And it's funny—you can always tell when it's time to shift gears and change hats. The frown gets deeper . . . the inner spirit gets irritable . . . the jaw gets set . . . the mind gets fatigued—these are God's signals to you that say, "Don't abort, divert! Don't cave in, get away! Don't crumble, create!" The saddest believers I know—those most bored, most lonely, most miserable, most filled with self-pity—are those who have never developed interests outside the realm of their work.

The only vision they possess is *tunnel vision*, the most significant thing they've ever created is an *ulcer*, the only thing they can discuss in depth is their old nine-to-five routine. No thanks! That's not a career, it's a sentence. It may be fulfilling the demands of an occupation, but you'll never convince me it's the experience of "abundant life" our Lord talked about.

Ladies and girls, sit down this very evening and read Proverbs 31:10-31. This passage describes a woman of great worth—a valuable human being. The interesting thing to note is that she has such balance. She is *not* locked into the dull demands of a routine existence. She is notably efficient in several areas *outside* the home and *beyond* the church.

Men, give attention to such characters as Nehemiah

or Job (when he was healthy) or David or Paul. Mark these names down on the ledger of guys who recognized the value and joy of involvement and accomplishment outside the boundaries of their "stated" occupations. One used his hands in construction, another composed music, another raised cattle.

Before you shelve this discussion, try answering these questions:

> Can you name at least one area of interest (outside the limits of your "calling") which you are presently developing?
>
> Do you experience as much satisfaction in your diversion as you do in your occupation (sometimes more!)?
>
> Whenever you plunge intoyour diversion, is it without guilt and without anxiety?
>
> Are you aware that your diversion is as significant to God and to your own happiness as your actual vocation?

If your answer to any of the above is no, you need a few splinters in your thumb. They may help you forget the worries in your head.

Deepening Your Roots

1 Samuel 16:18-23; 2 Samuel 22:1; Proverbs 31:1-31

Branching Out

1. Spend at least three hours this week on one of your hobbies, or finding one!
2. Start a new hobby that forces you to be with new people.

Orderliness

Doing all things "decently and in order" applies to a lot more areas than theology. It's remarkable how many guys who have the ability to articulate the most exacting nuances of their expertise never get their desks cleared off. The last time a lot of them picked up their socks was when they were finishing a week at summer camp. They're brainy enough to understand Einstein's law of relativity or figure out the answers to computer foul-ups . . . but the trash under the kitchen sink can overflow until it's ankle deep without their awareness. Isn't it amazing how many men have quiz-kid heads and pigpen habits?

And it's not limited to the male species. Some women have the toughest time just keeping a path clear from the front door to the den. I heard last week about a gal who was such a lousy housekeeper *Good Housekeeping* canceled her subscription!

She must have been a friend of Erma Bombeck. Erma's the one who says that her idea of being organized is hauling in the garden hose before winter. She's the one who admits that her cupboard shelves are lined with newspapers that read MALARIA STOPS WORK ON THE CANAL.

Of course, it's possible to become a "neatness neurotic." Like the fastidious wife of that poor fella who got hungry late one night and got out of bed for a midnight snack. When he came back to bed, she had it made.

Certainly there are ridiculous extremes. People who can't stand having a thing out of place are as bad off (maybe worse!) as those whose family at supper time resembles a Chinese fire drill. The answer to disorderliness is not vacuuming four times a day or running around the house nervously clicking off lights and tightening faucets or setting up your monthly bills according to the Dewey Decimal System. They put folks away who must have things that perfect. Furthermore, nobody likes to be around an individual so super structured. Once again—the secret is *balance*.

If the truth could be told, however, most of us don't struggle with being TOO orderly. Our problem is the other side of the coin. And the result is predictable: We burn up valuable energy and lose precious time because of it. Spending what it takes to become a littlemore efficient is an investment that pays rich dividends. Because we are reluctant to do so, our lives are marked by mediocrity, haphazardness, and puttingout needless fires.

Stop and think that over. Maybe a few questions will help prime the pump of self-analysis:

- Do you often lose things?
- Are you usually late for appointments and meetings?
- Do you put off doing your homework until late?

- Are you a time waster . . . like on the phone or with TV?
- Is your reading limited to only the essentials rather than heavier works?
- Are you prompt in paying bills and answering mail?
- Is your attire attractive? Things match? Clothing pressed? Shoes shined?
- Many unfinished projects lying around?
- Does your desk *stay* cluttered? How about the tops of tables and counters?
- Can you put your hands on important documents right away?
- Do you have a will? Is it in a protected place?
- Can you concentrate and think through decisions in a logical, well-arranged manner?

Stab, stab. Twist, twist. Even though those questions hit below the belt, they reveal the pulse of your efficiency heartbeat. Before you get all hot and bothered, fearing some gigantic plan only an efficiency expert with a master's in business could pull off, relax. If you're like me, life is too busy to add some unrealistic,humongous program.

Let's deal with the problem in a simplified manner. First off, admit to yourself that you could stand a change here and there. Try to be specific enough to pinpoint a couple of particular areas that keep bugging you. Don't bite off too much, just one or two trouble spots you plan to deal with first.

Now then, *write down* your problem. Maybe it would be:

I am usually late to a meeting. More often than not, I

have to hurry . . . and even then, I am five to ten minutes late.

Once this is done, think about several practical ways you can conquer the habit pattern you've fallen into. Again, *write down* the plan for correction. One final suggestion—work on only one or two projects a month. Too many targets will frustrate you. Don't forget to pray, by the way.

Proverbs is a book that puts a high priority on orderliness. We can't read it without getting motivated . . . and convicted! Take 24:30-34, where inefficiency is personified as a "sluggard."

> I passed by the field of the sluggard, and by the vineyard of the man lacking sense; and behold, it was completely overgrown with thistles, its surface was covered with nettles, and its stone wall was broken down. When I saw, I reflected upon it; I looked, and received instruction. "A little sleep, a little slumber, a little folding of the hands to rest," then your poverty will come as a robber, and your want like an armed man.

How can this happen to us? The answer is given a couple of chapters later:

> The sluggard says, "There is a lion in the road! A lion is in the open square!" As the door turns on its hinges, so does the sluggard on his bed. The sluggard buries his hand in the dish; he is weary of bringing it to his mouth again. The sluggard is wiser in his own eyes than seven men who can give a discreet answer (26:13-16).

The syndrome is painfully clear:

1. We see danger . . . but we don't care (the lion).

2. We are concerned . . . but too lazy to change (the bed).
3. We become victims of habit (the dish).
4. We rationalize around our failures.

"Decently and in order." That's our goal, remember. Most of us are a lot more decent than we are orderly. Which means we qualify as highly moral, modestly clothed, well-behaved sluggards.

Deepening Your Roots

1 Corinthians 14:40; Colossians 2:1-7

Branching Out

1. Take one of the items I asked you to "stop and think over," and make it an area you'll work on this week.
2. Identify two "messy" areas in your home. Choose one of them and clean it up by Sunday.

Impatience

As I write this I'm at 35,000 feet. It's 5:45 p.m., Saturday. It should be 4:15. The airliner was an hour and a half late. People are grumpy. Some are downright mad. Stewardesses are apologizing, promising extra booze to take off the edge. To complicate matters, a Japanese man across the aisle from me has a rather severe nosebleed and they're trying to instruct the poor chap . . . *but he doesn't speak a word of English!*

So now the meal is late. The lady on my left has a cold and makes an enormous sound when she sneezes (about every ninety seconds—I've timed her). It's something like a dying calf in a hail storm or a bull moose with one leg in a trap. Oh, one more thing. The sports film on golf just broke down and so did the nervous systems of half the men on board. It's a zoo!

It all started with the *delay*. "Mechanical trouble," they said. "Inexcusable," responded a couple of passengers. Frankly, I'd rather they fix it before we leave than decide to do something about it en route. But we Americans don't like to wait. Delays are irritating. Aggravating. Nerve-jangling. With impatient predictability we are consistently—and I might add *obnoxiously*—demanding. We want what we want *when* we want it. Not a one of us finds a delay easy to accept.

Do you question that? Put yourself into these situations:

● You're at the grocery story. Busy evening ahead. Long lines. Shopping cart has a wheel that drags. You finally finish and choose a stall with only two ahead of you. The checker is new on the job . . . her hands tremble . . . beads of perspiration dot her brow. Slowly she gets to you. Her cash register tape runs out. She isn't sure how to change it. You're delayed. How's your response?

● It's dinner-out-with-the-family night. That special place. You've fasted most of the day so you can gorge tonight. You're given a booth and a menu but the place is terribly busy and two waitresses short. So there you sit, hungry as a buffalo in winter with a glass of water and a menu you've begun to gnaw on. You're delayed. How's your response?

● You're a little late to work. The freeway's full so you decide to slip through traffic using a rarely-known shortcut only Daniel Boone could have figured out. You hit all green lights as you slide around trucks and slow drivers. Just about the time you start feeling foxy, an ominous clang, clang, clang strikes your ears. A train! You're delayed. How's your respond?

The rubber of Christianity meets the road of proof at just such intersections in life. As the expression goes, our faith is "fleshed out" at times like that. The best test of my Christian growth occurs in the mainstream of life, not in the quietness of my study. *Anybody* can walk in victory when surrounded by books, silence, and the warm waves of sunshine splashing through the window. But those late takeoffs, those grocery lines, those busy restaurants, those trains! That's where faith is usually "flushed out."

The stewardess on this plane couldn't care less that I'm a "pretribulational rapturist." Your waitress will not likely be impressed that you can prove the authorship of the Pentateuch. Nor will the gal at the checkstand stare in awe as you inform her of the distinctive characteristics of biblical infallibility which you embrace.

One quality, however—a single, rare virtue scarce as diamonds and twice as precious—will immediately attract them to you and soften their spirits. That quality? The ability to accept delay graciously. Calmly. Quietly. Understandingly. With a smile. If the robe of purity is far above rubies, the garment of patience is even beyond that. Why? Because its threads of unselfishness and kindness are woven on the Lord's loom, guided within our lives by the Spirit of God. But, alas, the garment seldom clothes us!

Remember the verse?

> But the fruit of the Spirit is love, joy, peace . . .

And what else? The first three are the necessary style along with the buttons and zipper of the garment. The rest give it color and beauty:

> . . . patience, kindness, goodness, faithfulness, gentleness, self-control . . . (Galatians 5:22-23).

The ability to accept delay. Or disappointment. To smile back at setbacks and respond with a pleasant, understanding spirit. To cool it while others around you curse it. For a change, I refused to be hassled by today's delay. I asked God to keep me calm and cheeful, relaxed and refreshed. Know what? He did. He *really* did! No pills! No booze. No hocus-pocus. Just relaxing in the power of Jesus.

I can't promise you that others will understand. You see, I've got another problem now. Ever since takeoff I've been smiling at the stewardess, hoping to encourage them. Just now I overheard one of them say to the other, "Watch that guy wearing glasses. I think he's had too much to drink."

Deepening Your Roots

Proverbs 14:29; Proverbs 19:11; Romans 12:9-13; 2 Corinthians 6:1-13; Ephesians 4:1-3

Branching Out

1. When you wait in line this week, offer to let the person behind you go ahead of you, or give a compliment to the person waiting on you behind the counter or checkout area.
2. As you wait to see the doctor, or to get a check cashed, or car filled with gasoline, etc., use those minutes to do some creative thinking rather than add fuel to your anger. Think about twenty things you can be thankful for. Here's one to start you off: (1) life!
3. When you are waiting for someone who is late take that time to *pray* for him!

When Following Seems Unfair

They were sitting around a charcoal fire at the edge of the Sea of Galilee. Jesus and over half of His chosen disciples. It was dawn; quiet and cool. Smoke drifted lazily from the fire as well as the aroma of freshly toasted bread and smoked fish. Perhaps the fog hung low. No doubt small talk and a few laughs occurred as they breakfasted. Surely someone commented on how good it was to catch over 150 fish so *quickly*.

The sounds of these hungry men must have echoed across the placid waters of Galilee. How delightful it must have been to know they were reclining on sand with the resurrected Savior in their midst.

Suddenly the conversation ceased. Jesus turned to Simon Peter. Their eyes met. For a few moments they talked together about the depth of Simon's love for his Lord. It must have been painful for the rough-hewn disciple, but he answered Jesus with honesty and humility.

Then, as abruptly as that conversation had begun, it ended—with a command. From Jesus to Peter. "Follow Me!" (John 21:19). Simple; easily understood; heard by everyone, especially Simon. The Lord wanted Simon's heart—without a single reservation. Jesus realized that His disciple was affectionately drawn to Him and greatly admired Him. But Jesus now told him to be totally available, fully committed with no strings attached. His command was perfectly calculated to get the fisherman off the fence.

Simon's response was classic. Verses 20 and 21 tell the story.

> Peter, turning around, saw the disciple whom Jesus loved (John) . . . [and] seeing him said to Jesus, "Lord, and what about this man?"

Isn't that typical? The finger was on Peter and he attempted to dodge some of its pointed direction by asking Jesus about John. "What about John, Lord? You're asking me to follow you . . . how about *him*? Aren't you going to give him the same kind of command? After all, he's a disciple, too!"

Notice Jesus' reply in the very next verse. It must have stung.

> Jesus said to him, "If I want him to remain until I come, what is that to you? You follow Me!"

This entire dialogue became permanently etched in Peter's memory. I am certain he *never* forgot the reproof.

Now what does this day to us—and what does it say to the members of our family? Simply this: Following Christ is an *individual* matter. The Lord saves us individually. He gifts and commissions us individually. He speaks to us and directs us individually. Peter momentarily forgot this fact. He became overtly interested in the will of God for *John's* life.

Does that sound a little like you? It may be that God is putting you through an experience that seems terribly demanding, even humiliating. You are facing the rigors of an obedient walk . . . and you may be looking over the fence or across the dining room table, wondering about *his* life, or *her* commitment. You're entertaining the thought, "It simply is not fair."

"What is that to you?" asks Christ. When it comes to this matter of doing His will, God has not said that you must answer for anyone else except yourself. Quit looking around for equality! Stop concerning yourself with the need of others to do what you are doing. Or endure what you have been called to endure. God chooses the roles we play. Each part is unique.

Some couples seem uniquely allowed by God to endure hardship—the loss of a child, a lingering and crippling illness, financial bankruptcy, a fire that levels everything to ashes, an unexplainable series of tragedies. While others are hardly touched by difficulty. It's so very easy for the Peter within us to lash out and bitterly lobby for an Equal Wrongs Amendment before the Judge. His response remains the same: "My child, just follow Me. Remember, you're not John . . . you're Peter."

Has God called you to a difficult or demanding mission field . . . or occupation . . . or type of ministry . . . or home situation? Has He led you to live sacrificially . . . or pass up a few pleasures? If He has—*follow Him!* And forget about *John*, okay? If Jesus is big enough to prod the *Peters*, then He is also big enough to judge the *Johns*.

Deepening Your Roots
Mark 1:14-20; Mark 10:21-31; Luke 14:25-35

Branching Out

1. Who or what do you usually blame for keeping you from following Christ? Decide to blame no one, or thing, but instead be responsible for your own commitment.
2. What sacrifices have you made in order to follow Christ? What new sacrifices are you confronted with today?

Better than Sacrifice

The bleating sheep on the slopes of Carmel brought a frown to Samuel's brow. The movement of oxen and donkeys in the sultry valley made his stomach turn.

But when his eyes fell upon two men in the distance, walking and talking together like friends, that was the last straw! As he approached them, he remembered his earlier instruction to Saul:

> The LORD sent me to anoint you as king over His people over Israel; now therefore, listen to the words of the LORD . . . "Now go and strike Amalek and utterly destroy all that he has, and do not spare him; but put to death both man and woman, child and infant, ox and sheep, camel and donkey" (1 Samuel 15:1, 3).

The words had been unmistakably clear and direct. King Saul was to carry out God's plans. It was an open-and-shut case of divine *extermination* without options and without opinions. The Sovereign of heaven had spoken . . . and there was to be absolute, instant obedience by King Saul. There wasn't. That's what angered Samuel when he visited the scene of slaughter and was met by the sounds and smile of life rather than the silence and stench of death.

With the severity of a submachine gun, the prophet faced the king.

"What's going on? Why do I hear and see these evidences of life? Who gave you the OK to erect a monument to yourself on the mountain? Where did you get the right to alter the command of God?"

Instead of admitting his disobedience, Saul stammered and stuttered three alternate routes:

First, he *lied*. "I have carried out the command of the LORD" (v. 13).

Second, he *rationalized*. "[We] spared the best of the sheep and oxen, to sacrifice to the LORD . . ." (v. 15).

Third, he *passed the buck*. "I did obey the voice of the LORD . . . but the people took some of the spoil, sheep and oxen . . ." (vv. 20-21).

Samuel was not impressed. He stared at King Saul and his buddy, Agag (who should have been a corpse by now), and then rebuked the stubborn king as few men in Scripture were rebuked:

> Has the LORD as much delight in burnt offerings and sacrifices as in obeying the voice of the LORD? Behold, to obey is better than sacrifice, and to heed than the fat of rams. For rebellion is as the sin of divination, and insubordination is as iniquity and idolatry. Because you have rejected the word of the LORD, He has also rejected you from being king (1 Samuel 15:22, 23).

Finally, we read Saul *confessed*, "I have sinned" (v. 24).

The sands of time have covered over this ancient scene, but our bent to disobey is still present. With this in mind, take a long look at Samuel's rebuke once again. In summary, he said three serious things to Saul:

- To obey is better than all sorts of sacrificial activities.
- To rebel is similar to involving yourself in demonism.
- To disobey is no better than worshiping an idol.

Powerful words! Let's apply them in a few details of life.

Has the Lord clearly led you to do something and yet you are saying "No" or "Not now"? Maybe you're trying to bargain with Him, substituting something else in place of His direct advice . . . like Saul. WAIT NO LONGER—OBEY!

Is there within you a stubborn spirit that causes you to rebel, argue, and fight back, even though you *know* it's against His leading? Perhaps you've bragged about your strong will or have cultivated the habit of resistance . . . like Saul. REBEL NO MORE—OBEY!

Have you developed the deceitful technique of hiding your disobedience behind the human masks of lies or rationalization or manipulation or blame . . . like Saul? DECEIVE NO FURTHER—OBEY!

The very best proof of your love for your Lord is *obedience* . . . nothing more, nothing less, nothing else.

Deepening Your Roots

1 Samuel 15; Proverbs 19:23; Proverbs 29:25; 1 John 3:21-24; 1 John 5:1-4

Branching Out

1. What's an area in your life you have a tough time conquering or letting God control? Next time you face that area, action, or thought, tell yourself, "I will not succumb. God I need Your strength to overpower this temptation."
2. Memorize one of the verses you read today that will strengthen your desire to obey God and help you resist Satan.

A Way in the Storm

Blow that layer of dust off the book of Nahum in your Bible, and catch a glimpse of the last part of verse 3, chapter 1:

> The way of the LORD is in the whirlwind
> and in the storm . . . (MLB).

That's good to remember when you're in a rip-snortin', Texas frog-strangler as I was a few weeks back. I nudged myself to remember God's presence as the rain-heavy, charcoal clouds hemorrhaged in eerie, aerial explosions of saw-toothed lightning and reverberating thunder. Witnessing that atmospheric drama, I reminded myself of its Director who was, once again, having His way in the whirlwind and the storm. Nahum and I took the Texas highway through Weatherford, Cisco, Abilene, and Sweetwater. There was no doubt but that the Lord, the God of the heavens, was in the storm. Nature refuses to let you forget her Artist.

But life too has its storms. Hurricanes that descend from blue, sun-drenched skies or clear, starry nights. What about the whirlwinds of disease, disaster, and death? What about the storms of interruptions, irritations, and ill treatment? If Nahum's words apply to the heavenly sphere, do they also apply to the earthly? Surely if God's way is in the murky, threatening sky, it is also in the difficult, heart-straining contingencies of daily living. The Director of the heavenly and earthly theaters is One . . . and the same. The cast may be different, the plot may be altered, the props may be rearranged, but just offstage stands the Head, the Chief . . . overseeing every act, every scene, every line.

Ask Nebuchadnezzar. He would reply:

> And all the inhabitants of the earth are accounted as nothing, but He does according to His will in the host of heaven and among the inhabitants of earth; and no one can ward off His hand or say to Him, "What hast Thou done?" (Daniel 4:35).

David, if asked, would answer:

> But our God is in the heavens; He does whatever He pleases (Psalm 115:3).

Paul would add:

> For it is God who is at work in you, both to will and to work for His good pleasure (Philippians 2:13).

Moses nailed it down with his comment:

> When you are in distress and all these things have come upon you . . . you will return to the LORD your God and listen to His voice (Deuteronomy 4:30).

Life is literally filled with God-appointed storms. It would take several volumes much bulkier than this one to list the whirlwinds in the walk of a Christian. But two things should comfort us in the midst of daily lightning and thunder and rain and wind. First, these squalls surge across *everyone's* horizon. God has no favorite actors who always get the leading role. Second, we all *need* them. God has no other method more effective. The massive blows and shattering blasts (not to mention the little, constant irritations) smooth us, humble us, and compel us to submit to *His* script and *His* chosen role for our lives.

William Cowper could take the stand in defense of all I have written. During one period of his life, heavy, persistent clouds choked out all sunlight and hope. He tried to end it all one bleak morning by swallowing poison. The attempt at suicide failed. He then hired a coach, was driven to the Thames River, intending to hurl himself over the bridge . . . but was "strangely restrained." The next morning he fell on a sharp knife—and broke the blade! Failing in this method, he tried to hang himself but was found and taken down unconscious . . . still alive. Some time later he picked up a Bible and began to read the book of Romans. It was there Cowper finally met the God of storms, submitting to the One who had pursued him through so many desolate days and windy nights. In the center of the storm, he found peace.

After a rich life of Christian experiences—but not without whirlwind and storm—Cowper sat down and recorded his summary of the Lord's dealings with familiar words:

ices
Up

ations. But the
upward the
e to a 1.1 per-
5 percent.
s the most-
ing 3/8 to 46 7/8
es changed

active blue-
o 5/8 at 104 3/8,
3/4 to 42 3/4,
2, General
nd AT&T

rted to be
Monday's
e black-

hange,
ading
nday,
ular
uses
l by
ng
ll

New York Stock Exchange

NEW YORK (UPI) - The following are complete closing nationwide composite prices for stocks listed on the New York Stock Exchange.

Tuesday, August 14, 1990

Stock	Div	P-E	Sales (hds)	Close	Net Chg.
—A A—					
AAR	.48	14	229	18⅜	— ½
ACMIn	.42	..	565	u9⅞	+ ⅛
ACMSc	1.26	..	699	x9⅝	...
ACMSp	.33	..	475	8¼	+ ⅛
ACMO	1.00a	..	208	g8	+ ⅛
ACMM	.33a	..	221	7½	— ⅛
ACMMk	.50	..	225	11¾	...
AL Labs	.16	20	1080	20⅞	+1⅛
AMIntl		2	352	2	...
AMR		11	9795	p49	—2⅛
ANR pf	2.67	..	66	25¼	+ ¼
ARX		15	108	u3⅛	...
AMEV	.35a	..	34	9	— ⅛
ARCO	2.50	11	1049	35½	—1½
ASA Lt	3.00a	..	4257	54	— ¼
AbbotL	.84s	19	4588	p41¾	+ ⅜
Abitibi	.50	47	15	x13⅝	+ ⅛
AcmClv	.40	9	471	8	— ¾
AcmeEl	.32	10	9	7¼	+ ¼
Acuson	s	24	294	44¾	— ½
AdExp	.48a	..	43	u15⅞	— ⅛
AdobeRes		17	19	u12⅝	— ⅛
AdbR pf	2.40	..	33	20¾	— ¼
AdbR pf	1.84	..	31	19¼	+ ¼
Advest	.16	70	99	3¼	...
AdvMicr		21	15289	p6	+ ¼
AdvM pf	3.00	..	5	26⅞	...
AetnaL	2.76	8	1540	46⅞	— ⅝
AffilPub	.24	18	215	9⅜	+ ⅛
ArrowEl		51	96	u5	...
Ahmson	.88	7	1584	17¼	— ⅜
Aileen		..	17	2½	...
AirPrd	1.44	13	2499	48¼	+ ⅝
ArbrnF	.30s	14	269	22⅛	— ⅞
Airgas		3	49	17½	+ ⅜
Airlse	2.52	9	14	17½	+ ⅛
AlaP pfS	.87	..	6	9⅜	...
AlP pfF	9.00	..	z50	94	—1
AlskAir	.20	10	368	u18¾	— ¼
AlbanyA	.35	13	624	12½	— ⅛
AlbrtoC	.20s	18	84	22⅞	— ⅛
AlbrtoA	.20s	15	82	19½	+ ¼
Albrtsn	.48s	22	1736	34⅜	+ ⅛
AlcanA	1.12	9	x6811	22¼	...
AlcoStd	.84	12	x198	32	+ ⅝
AlexAlx	1.00	18	206	21⅞	— ⅛
Alexdrs		50	214	36¾	+3⅜
AlgLudl	.88s	8	182	25½	...
AllghC	2.00i	8	4	81½	...
AllghItl	q	..	168	p 7-16	...
Allgl pfB	q	..	1	1	...
Allgl pfC	q	..	80	1⅞	...
llg Pw	3.16	10	700	36⅞	...
enGr		15	71	p16¾	— ¼
G pf	1.75	..	1	19	— ½
an	.30b	17	240	15¼	+ ⅛
	1.68	13	126	14¾	— ⅛
		..	49	u11¼	+ ⅜
		..	757	9⅞	— ⅛
			39	21⅜	+ ⅛
			64	u6	— ½
			34	33⅜	— ⅛
				10⅜	...
					...

Stock	Div	P-E	Sales (hds)	Close	Net Chg.
BrgKg	1.72a	12	51	13⅝	— ⅛
BurlCoat	s	9	122	u11½	— ⅛
BurlN	1.20	8	1983	31¼	+ ¾
Burl pf	.55	..	1	8	...
BurlRes	.70	36	1879	46¼	...
BurnPc	1.36	15	114	14⅜	— ⅛
Busnssld		6	2524	3⅛	— ⅛
—C C—					
CBI Ind	.60	22	242	39⅛	+ ⅜
CBS	4.40	16	481	178	— ⅛
CCX Inc		2	8	2¼	...
CDI		8	40	8⅝	+ ¼
CF Inc	1.00	..	145	3½	...
CIGNA	3.04	10	904	45⅛	+ ⅛
CignaH	1.08	..	224	6¾	+ ⅛
CML Grp		..	159	18⅜	— ⅛
CMS Enr	.40	8	934	31	+ ⅜
CMS Enhn		4	100	3¾	+ ¼
CPI Cp	.48	15	x137	27½	— ⅛
CNA Fnc	.24	7	205	73⅛	+1¼
CNA Inc	1.16	..	14	10	...
CPC Itl	2.00	18	1005	79¾	+1¾
CRIIn	1.08a	8	179	7⅜	...
CRS Sir	.12s	10	62	u13⅝	+ ½
CRI Lq	1.67a	10	196	12⅛	+ ¼
CSX	1.40	9	3557	33	+1
CTS	.75	8	28	21¼	— ⅛
CV RE	1.00g	7	107	5⅜	— ¼
CableW	.35b	17	532	27¼	+ ¾
Cabltrn		18	263	16⅛	— ¼
Cabt Cp	1.04	77	80	32½	+ ⅛
CabotOil	.16	..	54	16⅞	— ¼
Caesars Wd		8	1922	p14⅞	+ ⅝
CalFed	1.40	5	982	8⅞	— ⅛
Callahan		8	172	12½	— ⅛
Calmat	.40a	14	190	31⅞	— ⅛
Calton		3	169	½	+ 1-16
CampbRs		19	254	x¾	+ 1-16
CampS	1.00	144	758	p52½	+ ⅛
CdnPac	.92	11	759	16⅞	— ⅛
CanalCap		1	4	1¼	...
CanlC pf	i	..	14	1¾	— ⅛
CapCiti	.20	19	292	516⅛	+5⅝
CapHld	1.08	9	541	44¼	+1
Capstd	2.28	8	17	x14⅜	+ ¼
Cpst pfA	1.60	..	34	12⅛	...
Careercm		5	13	u1⅞	...
Carlisle	1.24	10	x63	32	+ ¼
Carolco		25	540	8¾	— ½
Carolc wt		..	261	2¾	...
CrFrght	.60	14	1090	16	...
CaroPL	2.92	10	942	42⅝	— ¼
Carpntr	2.40	10	75	47⅞	— ⅛
Carriage	.10	66	240	4⅝	+ ½
CartrH		85	1617	4⅛	— ⅜
CartWal	.92	15	140	50	— ⅜
CscNG	1.32	8	32	p15½	...
CastlCk		20	4042	p38¼	+ ⅞
Catrpllr	1.20	14	1316	47⅜	+ ¾
CedarF	1.25	6	219	11⅜	+ ⅛
Centel	.85a	63	1647	28⅝	+ ⅜
CntEnr	1.60	11	546	p17⅞	...
Centex	.40	8	294	32⅝	— ⅝
CentSW	2.76	14	413	39⅜	— ¼
CenHud	1.84	10	61	21⅞	— ¼
CnIllPS	1.84	10	9350	20⅞	+ ⅛
CnLaEl	2.56	10	55	34	+ ⅛
CnMPw	1.56	9	126	b18¼	+ ⅜
CnNws	.40b	14	384	16⅞	— ⅛
CentVt	2.08	14	40	24½	— ⅜
CntryTl	.42	35	277	25¾	+ ¾
Chmplt	1.10	8	9772	27	— ⅛
ChprlSt	.20	12	2	x8⅝	— ⅛
tHse		13			

Stock	Div	P-E	Sales (hds)	Close	Net Chg.
EKCO Grp		225	68	2⅛	...
ElPasR	3.00	..	10	21½	...
Elcor	.22	14	107	b7½	+ ¼
Eldon	.28	23	1220	21⅜	+ ¼
ElierInd	.28	13	307	12⅝	...
Elscint		25	659	2⅝	— ¼
EmergG		..	480	8⅝	+ ⅜
EmrsEl	1.26	13	9232	35⅜	+ ⅛
EmrsnRad		48	1363	3½	...
EmpDs	2.32	10	27	29⅛	+ ¼
Emprs	.68b	11	282	x21¼	+ ⅛
Energen	.94	14	120	16⅞	+ ¼
Englhd	.68	13	885	19½	— ¼
EnnisB	.72	12	483	19¾	— ¼
Enron	2.48	11	447	54¼	— ½
EnronOl	.20	124	62	24½	— ⅛
Ensrch	.80	26	1448	26⅛	+ ⅜
Ensr pf	7.90	..	1	72½	+1½
Entrgy	1.00	113	2737	19⅜	+ ¼
Enterra		33	569	20¼	+ ⅜
EnshEx	.30	32	2	x10⅝	+ ⅛
EnvrnSys		21	399	10⅞	— ⅛
EnvS pf	1.75	..	24	14¾	...
Equifax	.48s	22	825	17½	+ ½
Eqm pf	2.31	..	2	15½	...
Equimk	.16	2	510	3⅝	+ ⅛
EqtRlE	1.06	17	176	6⅞	+ ⅜
EqtblR	1.34	17	57	b39⅜	+ ¾
Equitec		..	3	¼	+ 1-16
Esterline		10	11	9¼	— ⅛
Ethyl	.60a	16	795	p29⅞	— ⅛
EuroFd		..	281	11¾	— ¼
EurpnWt		..	474	9	— ⅛
Excelsr	1.36	..	9	15⅜	...
Exxon	2.40	17	9384	52¼	— ⅛
—F F—					
FMC		8	534	35⅝	...
FMC Gl	.05b	17	2205	12⅛	+ ⅛
FPL Gr	2.36	10	1688	29½	+ ⅛
FabrCnA		12	187	18¾	+ ½
Fchl pf	3.60	..	1	34¾	...
FrfldCmnty		187	47	1⅞	...
FamDSt	.40	13	49	u12¾	...
Fanstel	.60a	12	238	12½	...
FarWstF		..	35	p1½	— ⅛
Farah		2	107	p3⅜	+ ⅛
FaysDr	.20	13	124	8⅝	— ⅛
Fedders	.48	8	2097	x10	+ ¼
FedExpress		18	694	38	— ⅜
FdHLn	1.60	9	1656	66½	...
FdMogl	.92	24	113	16¼	— ⅛
FdNtMt	.72s	9	9361	p33	— ⅝
FedNM wt	s	..	3456	p19	— ¼
FdPBd	1.00	4	527	18⅞	+ ⅜
FdP pf	2.87	..	36	39	...
FdRltlv	1.40	24	470	18⅝	— ⅛
FdSgnl	.66s	15	444	p26⅛	+ ⅛
Ferro	.64	15	666	25⅞	— ¾
FsCtBT	1.74	3	261	20¾	— ⅜
Fldcrest	.80	16	51	p10¾	+ ⅛
Filtertek	.44	14	3	u7½	— ⅛
Fingerhut		13	40	21	...
FsCapHld		3	698	3¾	— ⅛
FnvstF	.12b	..	837	5⅛	— ⅜
FsAmB	2.20	7	44	43¼	+ ⅛
FsBkSys	.82	14	172	x13¾	...
FBkS pf	2.62	..	21	g24⅞	+ ⅛
FBstnl	.90	..	201	g7⅛	— ⅛
FBosSt	1.20	..	74	8⅝	...
FstBrn	.04b	11	336	24	— ½
FstChi	2.00	9	1115	u24	—
FChi pf	6.00	..	5	5	
FChi pf	3.75	..	2		
FCtT pf	5.50	..	3		
FsFdBc	1.20				
FsF pf	2.15				
FstFnF					
FFc					

Stock	Div	P-E	Sales (hds)	Close	Net Chg.
HuntMfg	.31	12	595	12	
Hntngd	.23b	36	514	30	
HntwyPt	.40	..	33	4	
Hydrlc	1.60	10	77	2	
Hypern	1.20	..	272		
—I I—					
IBP	.60	18	425		
ICM	.48	..	115		
ICN Pharm		..	789		
IE Ind	2.06	12	88		
IMC Frt	1.08	11	1		
INA Inv	1.92	..	15		
IP Tm	2.88	7	10		
IRT Prp	1.16	18	64		
ITT	1.60	7	344		
ITT pfK	4.00	..	5		
ITT pfN	2.25	..	1		
ITT pfO	5.00	..			
IdhPwr	1.86	12	12		
IdexCorp		12			
IllPower		48	1		
IllP pfC	2.13	..			
IllP pfG	4.12	..			
IllP pfN	3.72	..			
IllP pfM	5.87	..			
IllP pfL	3.00	..			
IllTWk	.72	14			
Imcera	1.00	20			
IMO Inds	.50	7			
ImpC	4.91b	9			
INCO	1.00	6			
IndiaGrwth		..			
IndnEg	1.36	10			
IndiM pf	2.15	.			
IndoFd		.			
Ingrsoll	1.32	1			
InlndStl	1.40	2			
InspirRs	.12	7			
Intelogic					
Intelicall					
IntrRegionl					
IncapSc	2.10				
Interco					
Intrlake					
ItlAlum	1.00				
IBM	4.84				
ItlFlavr	2.16				
ItlMultf	1.1				
IntlPpr	1.6				
IntlRecvry					
ItlRctifr					
IT Corp					
IntrpbGr					
IntstJhn					
IntstPw					
Intst pf					
Intertan					
IwllGs					
IowaRs					
Ipalco					
IPCO					
IrshInv					
ItalyF					
Itel					
JHM					
JP					
JW					

God moves in a mysterious way
His wonders to perform;
He plants His footsteps in the sea,
And rides upon the storm.
Deep in unfathomable mines
Of never-failing skill
He treasures up His bright designs,
And works His sovereign will.

Before the dust settles, why not ask God to have His way in today's whirlwind? The play is so much more enjoyable when the cast cooperates with the Director.

Deepening Your Roots
Deuteronomy 4:27-31; Daniel 4:28-37; Nahum 1:1-3

Branching Out
1. Think back to a stormy time in your life. Did God use that storm to draw you near to Him, or show you something about His character?
2. Feel caught up in a whirlwhind? Name it. Ask God to have His way in your dustbowl of life.
3. Cut out a weather map from the paper and post it somewhere in your house to trigger your mind to think again of God and His sovereignty.

An Antidote for Weariness

It was about twenty years ago that my brother, now on the mission field, introduced a hymn to me I'd not heard before. He loves to play the piano—and plays it beautifully—so he sat at the keyboard and played the simple melody and sang the beloved words of a hymn I have since committed to memory.

The melodic strains of this piece often accompany me as I drive or take a walk in solitude or return late from a day of pressure and demands. Actually the hymn is not new; it's an old piece based on an early Greek hymn that dates as far back as the eighth century.

Art thou weary, art thou languid,
  Art though sore distressed?
"Come to me," saith One, "And coming
  Be at rest."
Hath He marks to lead me to Him
  If He be my Guide?
In His feet and hands are wound-prints,
  And His side.
Finding, following, keeping, struggling,
  Is He sure to bless?

Saints, apostles, prophets, martyrs,
Answer, "Yes."[2]

Surely in the home and heart of some soul who reads this book, there is a silent sigh, a twinge of spiritual fatigue . . . a deep and abiding weariness. It's no wonder! Our pace, the incessant activity, the noise, the interruptions, the deadlines and demands, the daily schedule, and the periodic feelings of failure and futility bombard our beings like the shelling of a beachhead. Our natural tendency is to wave a white flag, shouting, "I give up! I surrender!" This, of course, is the dangerous extreme of being weary—the decision to bail out, to throw in the towel, to give in to discouragement and give up. There is nothing wrong with feeling weary, but there is everything wrong with feeling weary, but there is everything wrong with abandoning ship in the midst of the fight.

Growing weary is the consequence of many experiences—none of them bad, but all of them exhausting. To name just a few:

We can be weary of *waiting*. "I am weary with my crying; my throat is parched; my eyes fail while I wait for my God" (Psalm 69:3).

We can be weary of *studying and learning*. "Of making many books there is no end, and much study wearies the body" (Ecclesiastes 12:12 NIV).

We can be weary of *fighting the enemy*. "He arose and struck the Philistines until his hand was weary and clung to the sword" (2 Samuel 23:10).

We can be weary of *criticism and persecution*.

> I am weary with my sighing;
> Every night I make my bed swim,
> I dissolve my couch with my tears.
> My eye has wasted away with grief;
> It has become old because of all my adversaries
> (Psalm 6:6-7).

Lots of things are fine in themselves, but our strength has its limits . . . and before long fatigue cuts our feet our from beneath us. The longer the weariness lingers, the more we face the danger of that weary condition clutching our inner man by the throat and strangling our hope, our motivation, our spark, our optimism, our encouragement.

Like Isaiah, I want to "sustain the weary" with a word of encouragement (Isaiah 50:4). Since our Lord never grows weary, He is able to give strength to the weary—He really is! If you question that, you *must* stop and read Isaiah 40:28-31. Do that right now.

But let's understand that God does not dispense strength and encouragement like a druggist fills your prescription. The Lord doesn't promise to give us something to *take* so we can handle our weary moments. He promises us *Himself*. That is all. And that is enough.

The Savior says:

> Come to me, all you who are weary and burdened, and I will give you rest. Take my yoke upon you and learn from me, for I am gentle and humble in heart, and you will find rest for your souls. For my yoke is easy and my burden is light (Matthew 11:28-30 NIV).

And Paul writes:

For he himself is our peace . . . (Ephesians 2:14 NIV).

In place of our exhaustion and spiritual fatigue, He will give us rest. All He asks is that we come to Him . . . that we spend a while thinking about Him, meditating on Him, talking to Him, listening in silence, occupying ourselves with Him—totally and thoroughly lost in the hiding place of His presence.

Consider him . . . so that you will not grow weary and lose heart (Hebrews 12:3 NIV).

Growing weary, please observe, can result in losing heart.

Art thou weary? Heavy laden? Distressed? Come to the Savior. Come immediately, come repeatedly, come boldly. And be at rest.

When was the last time you came to the Lord, all alone, and gave Him your load of care?

No wonder you're weary!

Deepening Your Roots

Isiah 40:28-31; 2 Corinthians 12:7-10;
1 Thessalonians 5:12-14

Branching Out

1. Set aside one hour today (make it a priority) and a place where youcan get away from everyone, from work, from noise, etc., and pour your heart out to God. Be honest.
2. Mark a day on your calendar (must be by next month) when you (your spouse may come, but no children) will take off (you cannot stay at home) and retreat somewhere to relax, read the Word, talk, pray, etc. Don't allow anything to interfere with this commitment. It's a must.
3. Find a way to relieve someone who is weary. Here are some ideas: babysit without charge, to allow a mother or father to shop or rest; help a friend finish a project; plant some flowers or weed a yard; mow a lawn or clean out a garage, etc.

Destination Unknown

Do you know where you are going?

The place? Dublin, Ireland. The time? Toward the end of the nineteenth century. The event? A series of blistering attacks on Christianity, especially the "alleged resurrection" of Jesus of Nazareth. The person? Thomas Henry Huxley.

You remember Huxley. Devoted disciple of Darwin. Famous biologist, teacher, and author. Defender of the theory of evolution. Bold, convincing, self-avowed humanist. Traveling lecturer.

Having finished another series of public assaults against several truths Christians held sacred, Huxley was in a hurry the following morning to catch his train to the next city. He took one of Dublin's famous horsedrawn taxies and settled back with his eyes closed to rest himself for a few minutes. He assumed the driver had been told the destination by the hotel doorman, so all he had said as he got in was, "Hurry . . . I'm almost late. *Drive fast!*" The horses lurched forward and galloped across Dublin at a vigorous pace. Before long Huxley glanced out the window and frowned as he realized they were going west, *away* fromthe sun, not toward it.

Leaning forward, the scholar shouted, "Do you know where you are going?" Without looking back, the driver yelled a classic line, not meant to be humorous, "No, your honor! But I am driving *very* fast!"

That true story is more than a story. It's an apt summary not only of the spirit of Huxley and his followers in the nineteenth century but of many in our own day. Great speed, much motion, rapid movement, but an unknown destination. As Rollo May, the contemporary psychologist, once admitted:

> It is an old and ironic habit of human beings to run faster when we have lost our way.

Maybe that describes you. It can happen to anyone—strong, aggressive individuals as well as quiet, passive types. Even people like Rabbi Saul. Back in the first century he, like Huxley, was engaged in a mission of assault. Bold, dogmatic, sincere, and scholarly, the Jew from Tarsus was busy putting Christians where he felt they belonged, out of circulation! Until . . . well, until he met the very Man he was trying to convince others was a fraud. The results? A changed life. A changed man. A changed mind. A changed mission. Even a changed name. Enter Paul the apologist.

Several years later he (of all people) stumbled into Athens (of all places). The scriptural record puts it mildly, calling Athens "a city full of idols." Pausanius, who wrote fifty years after Paul was there, states, "Athens had more images than all the rest of Greece put together." Pliny adds, "In the time of Nero, Athens had well over twenty-five to thirty thousand public statues.'' (He didn't include *another* thirty thousand in the Parthenon.) Petronius once sneered, ''It is easier to find a god than a man in Athens.''

By and by, monotheistic rabbi and polytheistic philosopher stood nose to nose in the ancient oval office of the world, the famed *Areopagus*. A lonely stranger facing an intimidating body of powerful men. Those eggheads had the appearance of brilliance. Like Huxley's driver, however, they didn't know where they were going. But they were driving *very* fast. In an impromptu speech of remarkable logic and brevity—a mere six sentences that takes only two minutes to read—the Jew became a Greek to the Greeks that he might win the Greeks. Read it for yourself in Acts 17:22-31.

After quoting (from memory!) one of their own poets, Paul referred to their ''unknown god'' and spoke not of Zeus but Jehovah . . . not about shrugging their shoulders at tomorrow *a la* the old Epicurean song, but about ''judgment . . . through a Man whom He (God) has appointed,'' having raised Him from the dead.

Boom! That did it. End of speech at Athens. Some began to sneer. Others mumbled, ''Mmmm . . . interesting. Let's meet again and dialogue together.'' Still others—perhaps only a few—stopped right then and there and believed in the One whom God raised from the dead.

In a big hurry these days? Driving yourself at breakneck speed? Working up lots of lather . . . but unaware of your destination? Easter is God's annual question. All across the world on Sunday morning Christ will lean forward and shout, ''Do you know where you are going?'' Wonder how many will be honest enough to answer, ''No, your Honor! But I am driving *very* fast!'' Perhaps many.

But a few will stop, turn around, and head toward the Son.

Deepening Your Roots
1 Kings 1:20-39; Proverbs 14:12; Acts 17:22-31.

Branching Out

1. Get up early and watch the sun rise, or catch a sunset in some quiet spot.
2. Now look again (in several Bible versions) at the sermon in Acts 17:22-31. Is the ''unknown God'' your God?

Loneliness

It is the most desolate word in all human language. It is capable of hurling the heaviest weights the heart can endure. It plays no favorites, ignores all rules of courtesy, knows neither border nor barrier, yields no mercy, refuses all bargains, and holds the clock in utter contempt. It cannot be bribed; it will not be left behind. Crowds only make it worse, activity simply drives it deeper. Silent and destructive as a flooding river in the night, it leaves its slimy banks, seeps into our dwelling, and rises to a crest of despair. Tears fall from our eyes as groans fall from our lips—but loneliness, that uninvited guest of the soul, arrives at dusk and stays for dinner.

You have not known the bottom rung of melancholia until loneliness pays you a lengthy visit. Peter Tchaikovsky knew. The composer wrote the following words in a minor key:

> None but the lonely heart can feel my anguish . . .

There is simply no other anguish like the consuming anguish of loneliness. Ask the inmate in prison this evening . . . or the uniformed man thousands of miles at sea or in some bar tonight . . . or the divorcee in that apartment . . . or the one who just buried his or her life's companion . . . or the couple whose arms ache for the child recently taken . . . or even the single, career-minded person who prepares a meal for one and goes to bed early, *alone*, surrounded by the mute memory of yesterday's song and today's disappointment.

I've crossed paths with many who could echo Tchaikovsky's lament . . . like the little Norwegian widow in Boston who now lives alone with only pictures of him whom God took . . . like the young nurse in 1967 who, after a shattered romance and broken engagement, went back to the Midwest to start over . . . like the alcoholic who wept on my desk one wintry morning clutching the bitter note left by his wife and kids: "Goodbye, forever" . . . like the husband beside the fresh grave on a windswept hill, who sobbed on my shoulder, "What now?" . . . like the disillusioned teenaged girl, away fromhome and heavy with child—wondering, "How can I face tomorrow?"

Some time ago someone placed this ad in a Kansas newspaper:

> I will listen to you talk for 30 minutes without comment for $5.00.

Sounds like a hoax, doesn't it? But the person was serious. Did anybody call? You bet! It wasn't long before this individual was receiving ten to twenty calls a day. The pang of loneliness was so sharp that some were willing to try *anything* for a half hour of companionship.

God knows, my friend, and He *does* care. Please believe that! He not only knows and cares—He understands, He is touched, He is moved. Entering into every pulse of anguish, He longs to sustain and deliver us.

In the strangling grip of Golgotha, our Savior experienced the maximum impact of loneliness. For an undisclosed period of time, the Father forsook Him. His friends had already fled. One had betrayed Him. Now the Father turned away. In the bottomless agony of that moment, our Lord cried—He literally screamed aloud (Matthew 27:45-46). The loneliness of those dark moments as our Savior carried our sin cannot be adequately pictured on paper. Cold print cannot convey it. But is it any wonder that He is now able to sympathize and enter in as we battle feelings of loneliness? Those who bear the scars of that silent warfare need no explanation of the pain—only an invitation to share in the sound and, if possible, help in the healing.

When we are lonely, we need an understanding friend. *Jesus* is the One who "sticks closer than a brother." When we are lonely, we need strength to keep putting one foot in front of the other—*Jesus* is the One "who strengthens me." When we are lonely, we need to lift our eyes off ourselves. *Jesus*, the "Founder and Finisher" of the life of faith, invites us to fix our eyes on Him (Hebrews 12:1-3) and refuse to succumb.

God is a Specialist when the anguish is deep. His ability to heal the soul is profound . . . but only those who rely on His wounded Son will experience relief. Jesus answers Tchaikovsky with these words in a major key:

> None but the trusting heart can feel My deliverance.

Deepening Your Roots

Psalm 25:16-22; Matthew 27:45-46; Hebrews 12:1-3

Branching Out

1. Consider someone you know who is possibly lonely. Call him up or go over and visit with him with the express purpose of "cheering him up."
2. Feeling lonely? Let's change that. Spontaneously drop by a friend's house and take the person out for pie and coffee, or breakfast (if it is early in the morning when you're reading this).

Be an Encourager!

Henry Drummond's remark haunts me at times:

> How many prodigals are kept out of the kingdom of God by the unlovely characters of those who profess to be inside!

Will you allow me in this private chat with you to pick out one "unlovely" characteristic frequently found in Christian circles . . . and develop it from a positive point of view? I'm thinking of the *lack of encouragement* in our relationships with others. It's almost an epidemic!

To illustrate this point, when did *you* last encourage someone else? I firmly believe that an individual is never more Christ-like than when full of compassion for those who are down, needy, discouraged, or forgotten. How terribly essential is our commitment to encouragement!

Woven into the fabric of the book of Acts is the quiet yet penetrating life of a man who is a stranger to most Christians. Barnabas emerged fromthe island of Cyprus, destined to an abstruse role of "minister of encouragement." In fact, his name means "Son of Encouragement" according to Acts 4:36. In comparison to the brilliant spotlights of this book—Peter, Paul, Silas, James, and Apollos—Barnabas appears as a flickering flame . . . but, oh, how essential his light was. How warm . . . how inviting!

Journey with me through chapter 4. The young, persecuted assembly at Jerusalem was literally "under the gun." If ever they needed encouragement, it was then. They were backed to the wall and financially stripped. Many were pressed, the needs were desperate. The comforter from Cyprus spontaneously gave all he had. He sold a track of land and demonstrated that he was living for others by bringing the proceeds to this band of believers (vv. 32-37). That's what we might call: *encouragement in finances*.

The next time Barnabas appears, he's at it again! In chapter 11 the Body is growing and the Word is spreading like a flame. It's too big for the leaders to handle. Assistance is needed: gifted assistance. What does Barnabas do? He searches for and finds Saul of Tarsus (v. 25) who was an outcast because of his former life. Not afraid to stick his neck out for a new Christian who was suspect in the eyes of the public, Barnabas took him by the hand and brought him to Antioch. Before the entire assembly, the "Son of Encouragement" gave his new friend a push into a priority position . . . in fact, it was into the very place where Barnabas himself had been experiencing remarkable blessing as a church leader (vv. 22-23, 26).

Without a thought of jealousy, he later allowed Saul to take the leadership and set the pace for the first missionary journey (chapter 13). It is interesting to note that the names were soon switched from "Barnabas . . . and Saul" (13:1), to "Paul and Barnabas" (13:42). This is the supreme test. It takes a great person to recognize that a man younger than he has God-given abilities and to encourage him to move ahead with full support. This we might call: *encouragement of fellowship and followship*.

The curtain comes down upon Barnabas' life in chapter 15. Journey 2 is about to begin. He and Paul discuss the possibility of taking John Mark, a young man who earlier had chosen not to encounter the rigors of that first missionary journey (13:13). Can you imagine that discussion?

"No," said Paul. "He failed once . . . he will again!"

"Yes," insisted Barnabas. "He can and will succeed with encouragement."

Paul would not withdraw his no vote. Barnabas stood his ground, believing in the young man's life, in spite of what happened before. Same style as always. You know the outcome (vv. 36-39). Barnabas demonstrated: *encouragement in spite of failure*.

Oh, the need for this ministry today! Is there some soul known to you in need of *financial* encouragement? A student off at school . . . a young couple up against it . . . a divorceee struggling to gain back self-acceptance . . . a forgotten servant of God laboring in an obscure and difficult ministry . . . ? Encourage generously!

Do you know of someone who could and should be promoted to a place of greater usefulness, but is presently in need of your companionship and confidence? Go to bat for him! Stand in his stead . . . give him a boost. He needs your *fellowship*. How about someone who is better qualified than yourself? You would be amazed at the blessing God would pour out upon you if you'd really back him with *followship*.

Then there are the failures. The Lots, the Samsons, the Jonahs, the Demases, the John Marks. Yes, they failed. They blew it. Are you big enough to extend a hand of encouragement and genuine love? Lift up the *failure* with encouragement. It pays off! It did in John's case. He wrote the Gospel of Mark and ultimately proved to be very useful to Paul's ministry (2 Timothy 4:11b).

To Henry Drummond's indictment, I suggest a solution. A new watchword for our times.

ENCOURAGEMENT!

Shout it out. Pass it around.

DeepeningYour Roots

Acts 4:32-37; Acts 13:1-39; 1 Thessalonians 5:1-12

Branching Out

1. Next time you go to church, sit by someone you don't know and ask God for an opportunity to speak an encouraging word, or invite him to eat with you at your home, or treat him to dinner.
2. Look for someone at work, or among your family, or a friend, who has failed. Rather than condemn the person, encourage him by believing in him and telling him so.
3. While everyone else finds fault in someone, you be different. Find something good to say to, or about, the individual.

Hidden Saints

Place: O'Hare Field, Chicago. Busiest airport in the world.
Time: Late Friday afternoon. Busiest time in the day.
Scene: American Airlines terminal. Busiest area in the building.
Location: Central concourse. Busiest traffic in the terminal.
People: Three preachers. Busiest mouths in the place.

Enter—one small, smiling airline stewardess who isn't too busy to notice a paperback copy of *The Amplified Bible* in one of our hands. "Hey," she shouted with a grin, "are you guys Christians?" "Yes, we are," we answered in unison. "Praise the Lord!" was her quick reply as hundreds of hurrying, preoccupied travelers brushed by. There we stood. having never met, we were suddenly one in the Spirit. Place, time, scene, location, people were reduced to insignificance as we stood together no more than five minutes and encouraged one another in the faith. Our earthly destinations were hundreds of miles apart—Buffalo . . . Tucson . . . Fullerton—but our eternal destination was identical. For one brief interlude we were locked together as family members . . . even though physical strangers. Then we were off on our separate ways.

Several unrelated Scriptures flashed across my mind following that encounter. First, I thought of God's announcement to Elijah when He mentioned 7,000 hidden, unknown yet available believers who had not bowed to Baal (1 Kings 19:18). Second, I thought of the unnamed, hidden saints in Caesar's household who never makde the headlines but were, nevertheless, counting for Christ (Philippians 4:22). Next, I remembered the long list of unheard-of Christians Paul listed in Romans 16—hidden saints like Junias, Ampliatus, Urbanus, Stachys, Apelles, Andronicus, Aristobulus, Phlegon, Hermes . . . and on and on (vv. 7-15)! You won't find a familiar name in the bunch, but they still belonged to the Savior.

Hidden saints—how many there are! Not insignificant nor reluctant, just *unknown* to us. If we could see as our Father sees, I'm convinced we would be amazed at the size of His family. If the spiritual iceberg were suddenly turned upside down and exposed for all to view, the magnitude of the Church He is building would literally take our breath away.

Isaac Watts caught a mental glimpse of such a scene after he had meditated on Psalm 72. He recorded his thoughts:

From north to south the princes meet
   To pay their homage at His feet;
While western empires own their Lord,
   And savage tribes attend His Word.
People and realms of every tongue

Dwell on His love with sweetest song,
And infant voices shall proclaim
Their early blessings on His name.

How short-sighted we are. How restricted in our vision. Our God has planted His people all over this globe. The iron curtain, the bamboo curtain, the prosperity curtain, the poverty curtain notwithstanding. He has His prepared and appointed instruments. As yet the shafts are hidden in His quiver, in the shadow of His hand; but at the precise moment at which they will tell with the greatest effect, He draws them out and launches them in the air. History—biblical and otherwise—is replete with illustrations of unknown, hidden saints emerging from the woodwork and etching their mark upon humanity.

In unpretentious fashion, in subtle ways, many reveal their spiritual identity to those who can decipher the code: an ICHTHUS on the back window or around the neck . . . a well-used Testament in the pocket or worn Bible beside the hospital bed . . . an attitude of forgiveness when an offense is committed . . . a spirit of acceptance when death invades. Ah, there are dozens of ways hidden saints are brought out of hiding, but more often than not, their identity is neither displayed nor acknowledged.

My point is a simple one: *We are not alone*. To be sure, we are not all alike nor in the majority. We never will be! But neither are we an insignificant, struggling handful of nobodies stumbling and groping our way through life. We may be overlooked, but we're not overwhelmed. We may be unknown, but we're not unnoticed. We may be outnumbered, but we're not outclassed. We may be hidden, but we're not lost.

Never forget, we're the ones who belong to the King.

Deepening Your Roots

Psalm 72: Romans 16:1-27; Philippians 4:21-22

Branching Out

1. Look for some hidden saints this week and note any that are new to you.
2. Have you been hiding on purpose? If so, take a step this week and let others know you are a Christian.

Watch Out for Fakes

A friend of mine ate dog food one evening. No, he wasn't at a fraternity initiation or a hobo party . . . he was actually at an elegant student reception in a physician's home near Miami. The dog food was served on delicate little crackers with a wedge of imported cheese, bacon chips, an olive, and a sliver of pimento on top. That's right, friends and neighbors, it was hors d'oeuvres *a la Alpo*.

The hostess is a first-class nut! You gotta know her to appreciate the story. She had just graduated from a gourmet cooking course, and so she decided it was time to put her skill to the ultimate test. Did she ever! After doctoring up those miserable morsels and putting them on a couple of silver trays, with a sly grin she watched them disappear. One guy (my friend) couldn't get enough. He kept coming back for more. I don't recall how they broke the news to him . . . but when he found out the truth, he probably barked and bit her on the leg! He certainly must have gagged a little.

Ever since hearing that story—it is actually the truth—I've thought about how perfectly it illustrates something that transpires *daily* in another realm. I'm referring to religious fakes . . . professional charlatans . . . frauds . . . counterfeit Christians who market their wares on shiny platters decorated with tasty persuasion and impressive appearance. Being masters of deceit, they serve up delectable dishes camouflaged by logical-sounding phrases.

Hey, that's smart! If you want to make a counterfeit dollar bill, you don't use yellow construction paper, cut it in the shape of a triangle, put the Lone Ranger's picture in the center, and stamp "3" on each corner. That deceives nobody. Deception comes in *convincing* fashion, wearing the garb of authenticity, supported by the credentials of intelligence, popularity, and even a touch of class. By the millions, gullible gluttons are duped into swallowing lies, thinking all the while they are digesting the truth. In reality they are underscoring the well-worn words of Phineas Taylor Barnum: "*There's a sucker born every minute.*"

> For such men are false apostles, deceitful workers, disguising themselves as apostles of Christ. And no wonder, for even Satan disguises himself as an angel of light. Therefore it is not surprising if his servants also disguise themselves as servants of righteousness . . . (2 Corinthians 11:13-15).

A glance at the silver platter and everything looks delicious: "apostles of Christ . . . angels of light . . . servants of righteousness." Through the genius of disguise, they not only look good, they *feel* good, they *smell* good! The media serves them under your nose.

Testimonies abound! Listen to some:

"This is new . . . it has changed my life!"

Others say, "I did what he said . . . and now God speaks to me directly. I see visions. I can *feel* God."

Over two million freely shout. "Eternity is *now* . . . materialism is godly. Getting rich is a sign of spirituality."

A larger band of followers claim, "We own nothing. Everything goes to the guru."

You find them everywhere. On street corners with little magazines, looking ever so dedicated to God. Staring up at the stars, discovering the future. Sitting in small groups on hillsides, eating canary mix, refusing to shave or bathe lest they interrupt their "communion with God." The platter is filled with variety! You find some attending religious pep rallies led by flamboyant cheerleaders in $800 orange suits and diamond-studded shoes. On the opposite extreme are mystical dreamers who prefer seclusion as they squat in silence.

They may have a "new" look—feel and taste like the real thing—but they are not. As Screwtape once quoted to Wormwood their father's couplet:

Old error in new dress
is ever error nonetheless.[3]

Which is another way of saying, "Dog food is dog food, no matter how you decorate it." Or, as Paul put it so pointedly, "They are false . . . deceitful . . . disguising themselves as apostles of Christ." They may not look like it, but they are as phony as a yellow three-dollar-bill.

Unfortunately, as long as there are hands to pick from the platter, there will be good-looking, sweet-smelling tidbits available. But some day, some dreadful day, the final Judge will determine and declare truth from error. There will be a lot of gagging and choking . . . and it will no longer taste good.

Nothing tastes good in hell.

Deepening Your Roots

Luke 21:5-19; 1 John 1:5-10; Philippians 1:9-11

Branching Out

1. How does Satan try to deceive you?
2. Ask God to help you be discerning in all your decisions today; to know what is *best*. Write down a decision you made today that you sought God's counsel on:

Clichés

I'd like to start a club. But not just any club. I've had the name and membership requirements for this particular organization tattooed on the underside of my eyelids for a long time.

It's going to be called a *DWAC Club*: Down With All Clichés! Getting in won't be easy. In order to become a member, you'll have to pledge yourself to a life of verbal discipline. You'll have to promise a bold breakout from the penitentiary of worn out expressions where you've been imprisoned for too many years.

But that's not all. You will have to promise to express yourself in fresh, penetrating ways to both God and fellow man. Before getting in line to join DWAC, let me warn you: The dues are high. *First*, you will have to put the torch to much of your "spiritual language," throwing into the bonfire your treasured list of pet expressions. *Second*, you will be required to stretch your mental muscles as you force yourself to substitute meaningful terms in place of religious-sounding ad lib.

Still want to sign up? A *third* bylaw insists that you learn to adjust to a world free from the security of such threadbare clichés as:

. . . lead, guide, and direct us
. . . I trust this will be a blessing to your heart and life . . . (yawn)
. . . just trust the Lord
. . . share my testimony
. . . bless all the missionaries
. . . wonderful message in song . . . (sigh)
. . . bless the gift and the giver
. . . shall we bow our hearts together?
. . . a time of food, fun, and fellowship . . . (zzzz)
. . . bless this food to our bodies
. . . ad infinitum, AD NAUSEUM!

Now wait—stop and think before you pick up rocks to stone me. Haven't you heard those weather-beaten phrases so long you could scream? Or worse—maybe you're so mesmerized or embalmed that you don't even hear them anymore. Christians seem to have developed the use of trite, hackneyed words and phrases into an art. *Cliché* is a French term, really. Originally, it meant "stereotype," and Mr. Webster defines stereotype: "To repeat without variation; frequent and almost mechanical repetition of the same thing . . . something conforming to a fixed pattern." Like a broken record . . . a pull-string doll with ten pre-recorded phrases . . . the ceaseless droning of parking regulations at an airport.

Our Lord once told the Pharisees they were guilty of using "meaningless repetition" when they prayed (Matthew 6:7). *Don't we?* Are we qualified to sit in judgment? On another occasion Jesus rebuked them for appearing and sounding righteous before men when they were inwardly full of hypocrisy (Matthew 23:27-28).

All right, which one of us is going to cast the first stone at those Pharisees?

Without wanting to sound like an ultra-critical heretic, I will name a few places where twentieth-century clichés abound:

- In stale, cranked-out testimonies, lacking relevance and fresh thinking.
- In public prayers, particularly in groups where we "take turns" around the circle, or in pastoral and pre-offering prayers.
- In religious radio and television broadcasts, especially when the announcer or preacher is unprepared, lapsing into his shopworn stock of religious jargon.
- In old sermons warmed over in late Saturday night's oven, served the next morning.
- In missions conferences, Bible conferences, men's conferences, couples' conferences, prophetic conferences, family life conferences, most all conferences!
- In answers to standard questions about God, the Bible, and doubtful things.
- In pat, "doctrinal advice" to the sick, sinful, and sorrowing.
- In weddings and funerals.
- In lengthy devotionals tacked on at the end of a "fun" gathering.
- In public announcements made during "opening exercises" (cliché!) and church services.
- In seasonal greetings at Christmas, Easter, Mother's Day, Groundhog Day, etc.
- In cranked-out invocations and benedictions.

Honestly, I am not condemning. *I am pleading*.

We are witness and spokesmen for the God of infinite variety, boundless creativity, indescribable majesty and beauty. We hold in our possession a white-hot message of hope, a pulsating invitation to approach a living Savior. Can we justify garbing this hope in faded sackcloth, delivering it in a predictable monotone? I am longing for those of us afflicted with anemic phraseology to step forward for a transfusion. I am asking for a frank admission that our assembly-line answers and stale statements are covered with the cobweb of tradition spun by the spider of laziness. Many of our words lost their impact years ago, suffering for decades from the public abuse of overuse.

Before five separate groups, one after another, Paul described his life and service for the Great King. Yet each time he stayed creative. You won't find a single cliché in the inspired record of the battered apostle's words (Acts 22-26). If Paul could do it, so should we.

At this point, I openly submit a confession. *Preachers are the worst offenders*. If $5.00 fines were issued for each cliché that escapes over the pulpit, most of us would be broke at the end of each month. So let's sign a pact together, and call it a mutual DWAC project, okay? I will do everything in my power to tune up my communications . . . if you will, too. Let's fumigate our phrases, destroying forever that plague of verbal locusts which threatens to consume the freshness of our all-important message.

All potential DWAC clubbers: sign that membership card today. I've got my pen out, too.

Deepening Your Roots

Job 15:3; Job 18:2; Matthew 6:5-15; Matthew 23:27-39; Acts 5:40-7:22

Branching Out

1. Pay someone $5.00 for every cliché you use in a two-hour time period.
2. Listen carefully to some children this week and catch a vision to be fresh and real. Write down the favorite phrase you heard one of them use.
3. Eliminate a cliché from your speech.

A Sheltering Tree

Shortly before his death, Samuel Taylor Coleridge wrote *Youth and Age* in which he reflected over his past and the strength of his earlier years. He wrote, for example:

> Nought cared this body for wind or weather,
> When youth and I lived in it together. . . .

But, to me, the most moving line in this quaint work is the statement:

> Friendship is a sheltering tree. . . .

How true . . . how terribly true! When the searing rays of adversity's sun burn their way into our day, there's nothing quite like a sheltering tree—a true friend—to give us relief in its cool shade. Its massive trunk of understanding gives security as its thick leaves of love wash our face and wipe our brow. Beneath its branches have rested many a discouraged soul!

Let ne name a few. Elijah was ready to quit. Depressed and threatened, he turned in his prophet's badge and wrote out his resignation. God refused to accept either. He gave him rest, good food, and a tree named Elisha—who, according to Elijah's own tesimony, "ministered to him" (1 Kings 19:19-21). In the analogy of Coleridge, Elijah rested in the shade of Elisha's "sheltering tree."

Paul had a similar experience. In fact, the trees in his life significantly sustained him. There was Barnabas who stood by him when everyone else ran from him (Acts 9:26-27; 11:25-26). There was Silas, his traveling companion over many an otherwise lonely mile (Acts 15:40-41). When you add Dr. Luke and Timothy and Onesiphorus and Epaphroditus and Aquila and Priscilla, you find a veritable *forest* of sheltering trees in that great man's life. Even Jesus enjoyed Lazarus, Martha, and Mary. Even *He* was refreshed beneath those sheltering branches from Bethany (John 11:5).

But of all the trees that God placed beside His choice servants, one human redwood looms the largest, in my opinion. David was hunted and haunted by madman Saul. The king's single objective was to witness with his own eyes David's corpse. Beween Saul and David, however, stood a sheltering tree named Jonathan, who neither shook nor shed in that precarious place. No matter how hard he tried, Saul could not chop down that tree! Loyal and dependable, Jonathan assured David, "Whatever you say, I will do for you" (1 Samuel 20:4). No limits. No conditions. No bargains. No reservations. Best of all, when things were at their worst, he "went to David . . . and encouraged him in God" (1 Samuel 23:16). Why? Why would he provide such a refreshment? Because he was committed to the basic principles of a friendship. Because "he loved him as he loved himself" (1 Samuel 18:1). It was love that knit their hearts together. The kind of love that causes men to lay down their lives for their friends, as Jesus put it (John 15:13). No greater love exists on this globe.

Beneath whose branches are *you* refreshed, dear reader? Or, dare I ask, who rests beneath *yours*? Occasionally, I run across an independent soul who shuns the idea that he needs such shelter, feeling that trees are for the immature, the spiritual babes, or those who haven't learned to trust only in the Lord. It is *that* person I most pity, for his horizontal contacts are invariably superficial and shallow. Worst of all, his closing years on earth will be spent in the loneliest spot imaginable—a hot, treeless desert.

So, then, let's be busy about the business of watering and pruning and cultivating our trees, shall we? Would I be more accurate if I added *planting* a few? Growing them takes time, you know . . . and you may really need a few when the heat rises and the winds begin to blow.

But I should remind you that a real, genuine, deep, solid friend is exceedingly rare. Either you're still looking through the forest . . . or, like me (thank God), you're enjoying shade and shelter today beside your God-given tree.

Deepening Your Roots

1 Kings 19:19-21; Proverbs 18:24; Proverbs 27:9-10

Branching Out

1. Do something special for one of your close friends this week.
2. Send a card to a friend and let him know you cherish his friendship.
3. Make something for a close friend which will be a constant reminder of your friendship. (Ideas: picture album, pillow, name plaque, painting, etc.)

The Law of Echoes

A young boy lived with his grandfather on the top of a mountain in the Swiss Alps. Often, just to hear the sound of his own voice echoing back to him, he would go outside, cup his hands around his mouth, and shout, "HELLO!" Up from the canyons the reply reverberated,
"HELLO . . . HELLO . . . hello . . . hello. . . ." Then he would call out, "I LOVE YOU . . . I LOVE YOU . . . I love you . . . I love you . . . I love you. . . ."

One day the boy seriously misbehaved and his grandfather disciplined him severely. Reacting violently, the child shook his fist and screamed, "I HATE YOU!" To his surprise,the rocks and boulders across the mountainside responded in kind: "I HATE YOU . . . I HATE YOU . . . I hate you . . . hate you . . . hate you. . . ."

And so it is in life. Call it one of the immutable laws of human nature. We get in return exactly what we give. It all comes back. Incredible echoes mirror our actions to an emphatic degree, sometimes in greater measure than we give. The results are often embarrassing, or tragic.

What was it Jesus once said? Luke tells us:

> Treat men exactly as you like them to treat you. . . . Don't judge other people and you will not be judged yourselves. Don't condemn and you will not be condemned. Make allowances for others and people will make allowances for you. Give and men will give to you. . . . For whatever measure you use with other people they will use in their dealings with you (Luke 6:31, 37-38 Phillips).

Let's call it the law of echoes. Tennyson said:

> Our echoes roll from soul to soul and grow forever and forever.

The law of echoes applies to a marriage. You want a wife who is gracious, forgiving, tolerant, and supportive? Start with her husband! It will roll from your soul to hers, my friend. As our Savior puts it, "Treat her exactly as you would like her to treat you." That's quite a promise. But it rests on quite an assignment.

The law of echoes applies to our work as well. The rocky canyons within the lives of others are ready to echo back the identical attitudes and actions we initiate. Want your associates at work to be cheery, unselfish, free from catty, caustic comments and ugly glares? The place to begin is with that person who glares back at you from the bathroom mirror every morning.

The law is remarkably consistent. Children echo their parents; pupils in a classroom are usually echoes of teachers; a congregation of worshipers is more often than not a reflection of the pastor. If the one communicating is negative, severe, blunt, and demanding

. . . guess what? The echo reflects those same characteristics, almost without exception.

I read recently about a teacher who asked her students to jot down, in thirty seconds, names of people they really disliked. Some students could think of only one persosn during that half minute. Others listed as many as fourteen. The interesting fact that emerged from the research was—*those who disliked the most people were themselves the most widely disliked*.

The law of echoes. If you want others to judge and condemn you, you start it. If you want them to be understanding, broad-minded, allowing you room to be you—then begin by being that way yourself. Like begets like. Smiles breed smiles. A positive attitude is as contagious as Hong Kong flu. Unfortunately, so are frowns, sighs, and harsh words. Whatever you deposit in the echo bank, you draw in return. Sometimes *with interest*.

A missionary was sitting at her second story window when she was handed a letter from home. As she opened the letter, a crisp, new, ten-dollar bill fell out. She was pleasantly surprised, but as she read the letter her eyes were distracted by the movement of a shabbily dressed stranger down below, leaning against a post in front of the building. She couldn't get him off her mind. Thinking that he might be in greater financial stress than she, she slipped the bill into an envelope on which she quickly penned "Don't despair." She threw it out the window. The stranger below picked it up, read it, looked up, and smiled as she tipped his hat and went his way.

The next day she was about to leave the house when a knock came at the door. She found the same shabbily dressed man smiling as he handed her a roll of bills. When she asked what they were for, he replied:

"That's the sixty bucks you won, lady. *Don't Despair* paid five to one."

Deepening Your Roots

Luke 6:27-42; John 8:15; James 4:7-12

Branching Out

1. What's the nicest thing someone could do for you today?
2. Go do it for someone.

Tomorrow

I was driving up to Forest Home with easy listening music crooning through the speaker. A quiet drive on a mellow Sunday afternoon. Then I saw something up ahead. Before I realized what it was, it flashed in my mind as something terribly wrong—out of place—distorted.

An overturned car—I could see it now. An ambulance screamed somewhere back. I felt like someone had pushed a fist into my stomach. Directing traffic around the accident, a highway patrolman briskly motioned on the crawling line of cars. I got too close of a look at the vehicle resting on its crumpled top. The scene hangs in my mind . . . the bystanders staring in open-mouthed disbelief . . . two men dragging limp bodies out of the wreckage onto the pavement. All of the passengers were either dead or terribly mutilated.

Such a warm, peaceful Sunday. The day was bright and filled with leisure hours. But for three people, that moment the world flipped—violently, crazily, fatally—upside down. What appeared to be another day of "fun-'n'-games" became a day of infamous calamity. Naturally, I wondered if those victims knew our Lord—if they could smile at eternity. My pulse shot up so that I had to grip the wheel with both hands. Under my breath, I mumbled Proverbs 27:1:

> Do not boast about tomorrow, for you
> do not know what a day may bring forth.

James 4:13-14 was certainly written with that particular proverb in mind. I said it out loud—several times—as the traffic resumed speed and scattered heedless across the afternoon.

> Come now, you who say, "Today or tomorrow, we shall go to such and such a city, and spend a year there and engage in business and make a profit." Yet you do not know what your life will be like tomorrow. You are just a vapor that appears for a little while and then vanishes away.

Sit down for a moment, please. Find a quiet spot in your dwelling, just for sixty seconds. Think—just think about the two statements: ". . . you do not know what your life will be like tomorrow . . ." and ". . . you do not know what a day may bring forth."

Man's knowledge seems impressive—awesome. We can split atoms, we can build skyscrapers, transplant kidneys, program computers, explore and explain outer space, and even unknot the problems of ecology. But when it comes to *tomorrow*, our knowledge plunges to zero. Whoever you are. You may be a Ph.D. from Yale, you may be a genius in your field with an I.Q. above 170, marvelously gifted and totally capable in any number of advanced, techological specialties—but you simply *do not know* what tomorrow will bring. Scientists may project, program, predict, deduct, deduce, and compute diagrams about the future. They're still only guessing. In algebraic terms, tomorrow remainss factor X . . . a mystery. It cannot be explained. It defies all attempts to be exposed. It lies hidden in the depths of God's unfathomable, intricately interwoven plan.He has not been pleased to unveil it until this old earth spins sufficiently to see the dawn. And then . . . only one moment at a time.

Tomorrow. It may bring sickness, sorrow, or tragedy. It may announce an answer to your waiting prayer. It may introduce you to prosperity, the beginning of a friendship, a choice opportunity for sharing your Lord . . . or just another twenty-four hours of waiting, trusting, and claiming His presence. It may not even come! God may choose this very day to intervene and take you Home—either by death or by Rapture. We can speculate, we can dread, we can dream—but we do not know.

This sort of thinking leads to an inevitable question: Are you ready? "Ready for what?" you may ask. "Ready for *anything*" is my answer. Is your trust, your attitude of dependence sufficiently stable to sustain you *regardless*? Remember Job's avalanche? Should your Lord be pleased to turn you into a Job, would He still be your Treasure and your Triumph? Don't let the answer slip off your tongue too easily. Think about the implications of that question to your own life, health, job, and family. Should your Lord make you an Enoch, would you be reluctant to make that eternal journey?

Thank the Lord, it is His *love* that arranges our tomorrows . . . and we may be certain that whatever it brings, His love sent it our way. That is why I smile every time I read Romans 11:33. Let it bring a smile into your world.

> Oh, what a wonderful God we have! How great are His wisdom and knowledge and riches! How impossible it is for us to understand His decisions and His methods! (TLB).

Deepening Your Roots
Proverbs 16:1-9; Proverbs 27:1; Luke 12:13-21

Branching Out

1. What plans do you have for tomorrow? Wait one day . . . then write in what actually took place.
2. On a calendar you use a lot, write one of the verses you read today and make an effort to incorporate it into your life.

Illogical Logic

The weather was bright and cheerful. The rays of a New Guinea sun burned down on a village normally occupied by the Tifalmin natives, but they were out in the field working on their farms and gathering firewood. It was a lazy Sunday afternoon. No one dreamed disaster was about to strike. Walt and Vonnie Steinkraus, a dedicated Wycliffe missionary couple, were at home resting alongside their daughters Kerry and Kathy.

At precisely 3:00 P.M., a freak of nature occurred. A huge section of the 300-foot mountain on the opposite side of the river from the Steinkraus's house suddenly broke loose. With a deafening roar and incredible force, a half-mile-wide, 100-foot-deep section plunged downward . . . scooping out sandbanks and crossing the river with lightning-like speed. It drove through the opposite bank and covered the village with rock, mud, and debris ten feet deep. The missionary family was buried in the landslide. Death was instantaneous. It's possible they never even heard a sound. Two eyewitnesses ran three miles to a mining camp and reported the scene. A Western Union telegram bore bleak news:

MARCH 21/71 URGENT! WALT AND VONNIE

STEINKRAUS AND CHILDREN BURIED IN VILLAGE BY LANDSLIDE SUNDAY 21ST. STOP. PLEASE NOTIFY NEXT OF KIN. STOP. VONNIE'S FATHER HAS HEART CONDITION.

The news stung deep. A numbing disbelief gripped relatives and friends across America. The Wycliffe family was stunned, even though many were seasoned veterans, tempered for years in the fires of hardship and affliction. How wrong it seemed . . . how unfair! *Why?* With a world full of reprobates and rebels, why a missionary family? With a thousand other vacant hillsides many miles from a living soul, why that mountain . . . at that time? With pockets of people all over the island not half as strategic as the Steinkraus couple, why them? Engaged in the painstaking process of translating the Bible into the Tifalmin tongue, Walt and Vonnie were taken before the project was complete.

Forgive the way this sounds, but God's heavenly plan doesn't always make earthly sense. Candidly, His logic seems a little weird at times. Nobody likes to admit it verbally, but we all *think* it, right? His logic is illogical—to us, that is. Stop and think about that before you blindly toss it aside for fear of feeling like a heretic. What better answer do you have for those events in life that defy explanation?

- Like Job's boils, David's polygamy, the disciples' insensitivity.
- Or how about a knockout like Abigail getting stuck with a dummy like Nabal.
- How about the Lord's choice of Samson to judge the Jews.

- And the long period of time He let Saul harass David.
- We wonder about the trail of blood that consistently followed Paul.
- And the extent to which the wicked get away with murder.
- Why some babies are born health; others, deformed and damaged.
- Or—the family of six whose mother gets cancer.
- How about the number of religious charlatans that run free?
- And we can't forget the atrocities down through history:—like the senseless persecutions in the early centuries,—like the wholesale martyrdom of biblical reformers and saints,

—like the brutal extermination of six million Jews.
- What about the endless theological debates among reliable scholars?
- The inequity of a precious child beaten by a drunken dad.
- The reason God leads you to move just about the time you get settled.

Don't you wonder about such things? Not one is a nit-picking issue. Not one "makes sense." Try to square any one with *your* concept of logic and you wind up cross-eyed and tongue-tied.

Ready for another shocker? We're not supposed to have airtight answers! Why? Because our understanding is earthbound . . . human to the core . . . limited . . . finite. Our focus is from the ground up. Boxed in by the tight radius of *time* (as we measure it), multiplied by the circumference of *logic* (as we perceive it), we operate in a dimension totally unlike our

Lord . . . who knows no such limitations. We see now. He sees forever. We judge on the basis of the temporal; He, on the basis of the eternal. We try to make each piece fit neatly into the next one as we put the puzzle of life together, naming it Equity or Fair. Not God. His logic is inscrutable, unsearchable, unfathomable. The Creator needs no creature to interpret His way. His reasons. His style. His vantage point is infinity. *"It is too high, I cannot attain to it,"* admitted the psalmist.

And so, we *accept* rather than explain. We *trust* rather than try to make it all fit together so perfectly it squeaks. It helps to remember that each generation has only a few of the pieces, *none* of which may fit into one another. So stop trying to wrap everything in neat boxes.

Let's be illogical about this for a change. Otherwise, we try to play God's role. And most of us are fresh out of omniscience.

Deepening Your Roots

Isaiah 55:1-11; Psalm 73:1; 2 Timothy, 4:16-18

Branching Out

1. Write down something specific from your life that is hard to understand or that you question God about. Today, simply trust God with your "why" and allow Him to bring peace to your heart.
2. Name something in your life, or a part of your body, or in your surroundings, that cannot be changed. Now, answer this question: Have you accepted this unchangeable item even though you may not understand why God allowed it? If not, ask God to help you come to accept it, trust Him, and use it for His glory.
3. Name a person you know in a difficult stuation who has chosen to trust God rather than question him.

The Sting of Pearls

Got your yellow pad and pencil out? If not, just stop long enough to make a mental list of some of the things that irritate you.Here are a few suggestions that will get you started:

traffic jams	cold food	squeaking doors
talkative people	interruptions	incompetence
long lines	reminders	flat tires
crying babies	deadlines	balancing checkbooks
phone calls	nosy neighbors	doing dishes
misplaced keys	being rushed	mothers-in-law
untrained pets	late planes	weeds
stuck zippers	tight clothes	high prices
	peeling onions	

Any of those make you want to grind your teeth? Some of it sounds like today, doesn't it? It's easy to get the feeling that you can't win—no matter how hard you try. You start to entertain the thought I saw printed rather hurriedly on a small wooden plaque several weeks ago:

> I am planning to have a nervous breakdown. I have earned it . . . I deserve it . . . I have worked hard for it . . . and nobody's going to keep me from having it!

If it weren't for irritations we'd be very patient, wouldn't we? We could wade calmly through life's placid sea and never encounter a ripple. Unfortunately, irritations comprise the major occupational hazard of the human race. One of these days it should dawn upon our minds that we'll never be completely free from irritations as long as we tread Planet Earth. Never. Upon arriving at such a profound conclusion, it would be wise to consider an alternative to losing our cool. The secret is *adjusting*.

Sure, that sounds simple. But it isn't. Several things tend to keep us on the ulcerated edge of irritability. If we lived in the zoo, the sign outside our cage might read: "Human Being—Creature of Habit." We tend to develop habit reactions, wrong though they may be. We are also usually in a hurry . . . inordinately wedded to the watch on our wrist. Furthermore, many of our expectations for the day are unrealistic. Echoing in our heads are the demanding voices of objectives that belong to a *week*, rather than a single day. All of this makes the needle on our inner pressure gauge whirl like Mario Andretti's tachometer. When you increase the heat to our highly pressurized system by a fiery irritation or two . . . or three . . . BOOM! Off goes the lid and out comes the steam.

It helps me if I remember that God is in charge of my day . . . not I. While He is pleased with the wise management of time and intelligent planning from day to day. He is mainly concerned with the development of inner character. He charts growth toward maturity, concerning Himself withthe cultivationof priceless, attractive qualities that make us Christlike down deep within. One of His preferred methods of training us is through adjustment to irritation.

A perfect illustration? The oyster and its pearl.

Pearls are the product of pain. For some unknown reason, the shell of the oyster gets pierced and an alien substance—a grain of sand—slips inside. On the entry of that foreign irritant, all the resources within the tiny, sensitive oyster rush to the spot and begin to release healing fluids that otherwise would have remained dormant. By and by the irritant is covered and the wound is healed—by a *pearl*. No other gem has so fascinating a history. It is the symbol of stress—a healed wound . . . a precious, tiny jewel conceived through irritation, born of adversity, nursed by adjustments. Had there been no wounding, no irritating interruption, there could have been no pearl. Some oysters are never wounded . . . and those who seek for gems toss them aside, fit only for stew.

No wonder our heavenly home has as its entrance *pearly* gates! Those who go through them need no explanation. They are the ones who have been wounded, bruised, and have responded to the sting of irritations with the pearl of adjustment.

J. B. Phillips must have realized this as he paraphrased James 1:2-4:

> When all kinds of trials crowd into your lives, my brothers, don't resent them as intruders, but welcome them as friends! Realize that they have come to test your endurance. But let the process go on until that endurance is

fully developed, and you will find you have become men (and women) of mature character. . . .

Deepening Your Roots
Daniel 6:1-28; Job 23:8-12

Branching Out

1. If you are a woman, wear pearl earrings, a ring, or a necklace today to remind yourself of the process we all go through and that it is possible to endure adversity and come out the winner. If you are a man, find some item that can help you remember today's thought.
2. Adjustment. When your first irritation of the day comes along, quickly tell yourself: "God is in control" and mentally make the pearl of adjustment.
3. Decide to let God be in control of your day.Have fun by writing down on a three by five card what happens in the next twenty-four hours. Review the card before you hit the sack.

Bitterness

During my hitch in the Marine Corps, my wife and I rented a studio apartment in South San Francisco from a gentleman named Mr. Slagle. He suffered with a back ailment that was caused by an injury received in prison camp during the Second World War. Captured at Wake Island and later confined for years in China, he was left partially paralyzed when an enemy soldier struck him with a rifle butt.

When I visited with this landlord, he'd tell one story after another of how barbarically he'd been treated. With vile language and intense emotion, he spoke of the tortures he'd endured and of his utter hatred for the Japanese. Here was a man who had been horribly wronged—without question. The constant misery and pain he lived with could not be measured. My heart went out to him.

But there was another factor which made his existence even *more* lamentable. Our landlord became a bitter man. Even though (at that time) he was thirteen years removed from the war . . . even though he had been safely released from the concentration camp and was now able to carry on physically . . . even though he and his wife owned a lovely dwelling and had a comfortable income, the crippled man was bound by the grip of *bitterness*. He was still fighting a battle that should have ended years before. In a very real sense, he was still in prison.

His bitterness manifested itself in intense prejudice, an acrid tongue, and an everyone's-out-to-get-me attitude. I am convinced that he was far more miserable by 1957 than he had been in 1944. There is no torment like the inner torment of an unforgiving spirit. It refuses to be soothed, it refuses to be healed, it refuses to forget.

In the New Testament, every mention of bitterness comes from the same Greek root, *pic*, which means "to cut, to prick." The idea is a pricking or puncturing which is pungent and penetrating. We read in Luke 22:62 that Peter "wept bitterly." He wept because he was pricked in his conscience. He was "cut to the quick," we would say. In Acts 8:23, a man was said to have been "in the gall of bitterness" when he wanted to appear godly and spiritually powerful. He was simply a religious phony, bitter to the core.

Hebrews 12:15 states that a root of bitterness can spring up and cause trouble, causing many to be defiled. You cannot nurture the bitterness plant and at the same time keep it concealed. The bitter root bears bitter fruit. You may think you can hide it . . . live with it . . . "grin and bear it," but you cannot. Slowly, inexorably, that sharp, cutting edge of unforgiveness will work its way to the surface. The poison seedling will find insidious ways to cut into others. Ironically, the one who suffers most is the one who lashes out at those around him.

How can I make such a statement? Because of the

parable Jesus presented in Matthew 18. Find a Bible and read verses 21 through 35. The context is "forgiveness." The main character is a man who refused to forgive a friend, even though he himself had recently been released from an enormous debt he had incurred. Because of his tacit refusal to forgive, this bitter man was "handed over to the torturers. . . ." And then Jesus adds the punch line:

> So shall my heavenly Father also do to you, if each of you does not forgive his brother from your heart (v. 35).

Did you hear what He said? He said that we who refuse to forgive—we who live in the gall of bitterness—will become victims of torture, meaning intense *inner* torment. If we nurture feelings of bitterness we are little better than inmates of an internal concentration camp. We lock ourselves in a lonely isolation chamber, walled in by our own refusal to forgive.

Please remember—Jesus was speaking to His *disciples*, not unbelievers. A Christian is a candidate for confinement—and unspeakable suffering—until he or she fully and completely forgives others . . . even when others are in the wrong.

I can now understand why Paul listed bitterness *first* when he said:

> Let all bitterness and wrath and anger and clamor and slander be put away from you, along with all malice. And be kind to one another, tender-hearted, forgiving each other, just as God in Christ also has forgiven you (Ephesians 4:31-32).

For your sake, let me urge you to "put away all

bitterness'' *now*. There's no reason to stay in P.O.W. camp a minute longer. The escape route is clearly marked.

It leads to the cross . . . where the only One who had a right to be bitter wasn't.

Deepening Your Roots
Genesis 27:41-45; Matthew 18:21-35

Branching Out

1. Are you still bitter today over something that took place years ago? What is it? Are you ready to forgive that person (or maybe God)? Good!
2. Be quick to forgive someone today as you go about your work, chores at home, etc.
3. As a friend, or spouse, if he senses any bitterness present in you. If he says yes, deal with it today!

Stumbling

Nothing damages our dignity like stumbling!

I have seen people, dressed to the hilt, stumble and fall flat on their faces as they were walking to church. I have witnessed serious and gifted soloists, stepping up to the pulpit with music in hand, stumble and fall as the sheets of music sailed like maple leaves in an October breeze. I've watched a sure and winning touchdown by a fleet split-end—nobody within fifteen yards—foiled by a stumble. I've looked on as brides and grooms stumbled in unison . . . as bandsmen stumbled in formation . . . as shoppers stumbled in stores . . . as rigid Marine officers stumbled while inspecting the troops . . . as elite, elegant ladies stumbled on stage . . . as cap and gown grads stumbled to their knees receiving their diplomas . . . and as an experienced, well-respected, eloquent speaker stumbled and fell just before he began to speak. I could never forget that one because in the fall he cut his lip and delivered his entire address while wiping the blood off his face!

And can't you remember when you have stumbled? Nothing is more humiliating or embarrassing than spilling our dignity as we fall flat on our pride. The first thing we do is take a quick look around to see who might have noticed. We long to become *invisible*. Some of my stumbling experiences made me shudder just to call them to mind.

But do you know something? Almost without exception the response of onlookers is sympathy . . . identification with the embarrassment . . . mutual ache . . . a deep sense of inner support. In fact, the immediate response is to help the stumbler back to his feet. I cannot remember a single occasion when anyone who stumbled was held down or stepped on by those nearby. I recall that there was instant concern for their hurt feelings and their physical welfare. I also recall that everyone who tripped got right back on his feet, shrugged off the momentary humiliation, and forged ahead. There's something to be learned, my friend, in all this business of stumbling.

In the penetrating letter of James, every verse is like a scalpel—cutting deep incisions in our conscience. Hidden within James 3:2 is something we often forget:

> For we all stumble in many ways.

What's he saying? Nobody's perfect . . . to stumble is normal . . . a fact of life . . . an act that guarantees our humanness. He goes on to mention that we often stumble in what we *say*. When it comes to the tongue, we blow it! He says (in 2:10) that stumbling brings guilt . . . even if it is in one, small area. Isn't that the truth!

Perhaps you have *just* stumbled as you read this today. You feel guilty, you feel like a failure. You wish like crazy you had never opened your mouth . . . or done what you did . . . or responded like that. You're miserable, discouraged, and you'd like to hide, or better still—crawl off and die. Ridiculous! Get up out of that pool of self-pity, brush off the dirt with the promise of God's forgiveness—and move on!

Now I must add a word of realism. Instead of receiving the normal reaction of concern and support, you may find that some who saw you fall will want to hold you down or bad-mouth you because you slipped. Ignore them completely! They have forgotten that James 3:2 includes *them*. The only difference is that you didn't get to see them stumble. But they have, believe me, they have.

What all this adds up to is not difficult to discover:

GOD WANTS TO USE YOU—STUMBLING
AND ALL—BUT HE WON'T DO SO
IF YOU REFUSE TO GET UP.

Stumblers who *give* up are a dime a dozen. In fact, they're useless.

Stumblers who *get* up are rare. In fact, they're priceless.

Deepening Your Roots

Psalm 37:23-24; Hebrews 4:12-16

Branching Out

1. See someone stumble lately? How did you treat him? Talk or laugh about him? Remember James 2? How about empathizing with the person?
2. Keep track of people who stumble this week and note how you reacted to each one.

Comforting

Two elementary-school boys were, for the first time in their lives, absolutely still. Deathly still. In separate pools of blood, each under a pale blanket, they awaited the arrival of the coroner. For them, school ended prematurely. With crushing authority, the grim reaper visited the vast metropolis of Los Angeles at the corner of Beach Boulevard and Rosecrans Avenue—unannounced and uninvited. In heavy traffic. In broad daylight. Death the Dictator came, saw, and conquered. He always does, which prompted George Bernard Shaw to write:

> The statistics on death are quite impressive. One out of one people die.

But what about those who *live on*? Those who try to pick up the jagged pieces? As I stood there beside my oldest son, fighting back tears, trying to swallow that knot in my throat, I kept thinking about two families that would never be the same. Two mothers and dads, especially. I could paint a portrait of the coming days: indescribable sorrow, disillusionment, sleepless nights, endless reminders, paralyzing anxiety, that unendurable sense of loss, that numbing mixture of anger, helplessness, denial, and confusion.

Let's pause here and pretend. Let's pretend you are the neighbor. One of those two grieving families lives next door. On an average Thursday afternoon, your phone rings . . . or a knock comes at the door. The information you hear stuns you. You're suddenly reeling, and you feel as if you're in a dream ("nightmare" might be a better word). Life screams to a halt. Thursday seems strangely sacred, almost eerie.

The grief of someone very near becomes so real you can taste it. The pain stabs deep and perhaps your first thought is, "Oh, how my heart goes out to——!" Your second thought is, "What can I do to help? What would be the best expression of love, compassion, and sympathy?"

Suddenly, you're stuck. There's no set of rules to follow—no handbook for showing mercy. You hurriedly thumb through your Bible and find no sermon notes on "How to Sympathize." No, my friend, comfort for the sorrowing cannot be regulated and systematized. To go through programmed motions with the grieving turns you into a good candidate for another "Job's counselor" . . . and none of us wants that title. What *can* you do? What *should* you do . . . or not do? What could be said that might be appreciated and appropriate?

Be real. As you reach out, admit your honest feelings to your friends. If the news stunned you, say so. If you suddenly feel tears coming, cry. If you are overwhelmed with pity and compassion, admit it. You may be a Christian with a firm hope in a life hereafter, but you're also human. Don't hide that. It may be through that gate a path of friendship will develop.

Be quiet. Your presence, not your words, will be most appreciated. The thick mantle of grief has fallen upon your friend, bringing dark, unexplainable sorrow. An abundance of words and attempts to instruct will only reveal an insensitive spirit to the grieving. The Joe Baylys, in the course of several years, lost three of their children. In his book, *The Last Thing We Talk About*, he shares his honest feelings when one of the children died:

> I was sitting, torn by grief. Someone came and talked to me of God's dealing, of why it happened, of hope behond the grave. He talked constantly. He said things I knew were true.
>
> I was unmoved, except to wish he'd go away. he finally did.
>
> Another came and sat beside me. He didn't talk. He didn't ask me leading questions. He just sat beside me for an hour and more, listened when I said something, answered briefly, prayed simply, left.
>
> I was moved. I was comforted. I hated to see him go.

Be supportive. Those who comfort must have a tender heart of understanding. They don't come to quote verses or leave a stack of literature. They come simply to say they care. Nor do they attempt to erase today's hurt by emphasizing tomorrow's hope. They are committed to the support, the understanding of the grieving. Few things heal wounded spirits better than the balm of a supportive embrace.

> A little girl lost a playmate in death and one day reported to her family that she had gone to comfort the sorrowing mother. "What did you say?" asked her father. "Noth-

ing," she replied, "I just climbed up on her lap and cried with her."

That's being supportive.

Be available. Everybody comes around the first day or two. But what about a month later? After the flowers? Or five months later. After the grass grows over the grave? Life, like the muddy Mississippi, keeps rolling along. Unfortunately, so do the memories of that little fella whose place at the supper table remains vacant. If ever the comforting hand of a friend is needed, it is then—when *other* kids are going swimming and snitching cookies and riding bikes. Be committed to comforting later on as well as now. Your appropriate suggestions that will help them break the spell of grief (C.S. Lewis wrote of "the laziness of grief") will help them begin again.

Like Jesus with the sisters of Lazarus in the crucible of grief, be real (He wept), be quiet (He took their angry rebukes), be supportive (He was deeply moved), be available (He stayed by their side). No big sermons, no leaflets, no attempts to correct their misunderstandings, not even a frown that suggested disapproval. He let grief run its course. Our Lord believed, as we should, that we are healed of grief only when we express it to the full.

Perhaps this explains why so many are grieving . . . and so few are comforting.

Deepening Your Roots
2 Samuel 1:17-27; John 11-17-44; John 16:5-22

Branching Out

1. What is the one thing you can do for someone you know who is grieving? Do it.
2. Rather than sending a sympathy card or sending flowers to someone experiencing grief, do something different to show you care. For example, consider sending Christine Wyrtzen's album, *For Those Who Hurt*, or sending a book, or writing a letter about how much the person means to you, or sending a tea cup and saucer with a note saying, "I wish I could be there to care for you during your painful hours."
3. Embrace (hug) someone today and reassure him of your concern for him—regardless of whether he is experiencing grief or not.

Call for Help!

A PRAYER TO BE SAID
WHEN THE WORLD HAS GOTTEN YOU DOWN,
AND YOU FEEL ROTTEN,
AND YOU'RE TOO DOGGONE TIRED TO PRAY,
AND YOU'RE IN A BIG HURRY,
AND BESIDES, YOU'RE MAD AT EVERYBODY . . .
help.

There it was. One of those posters. Some are funny. Some are clever. Others beautiful. A few, thought-provoking. This one? Convicting. God really wanted me to get the message. He nudged me at a Christian conference center recently when I first read it in an administrator's office. A few weeks and many miles later He shot me the signal again—I practically ran into the same poster in a friend's office. Then just last week, while moving faster than a speeding bullet through a Portland publishing firm, I came face to face with it *again*. But this time the message broke through my defenses and wrestled me to the mat for the full count.

"My son, slow down. Ease back. Admit your needs."

Such good counsel. But so tough to carry out. Why is that? Why in the world is it such a struggle for us to cry out for assistance?

- Ants do it all the time and look at all *they* achieve.
- In my whole life I have never seen a football game won without substitutions.
- Even the finest of surgeons will arrange for help in extensive or delicate operations.
- Highway patrolmen travel in pairs.
- Through my whole career in the Marine Corps I was drilled to dig a foxhole for *two* in the event of battle.

Asksing for help is smart. It's also the answer to fatigue and the "I'm indispensable" image. But something keeps us from this wise course of action, and that something is *pride*. Plain, stubborn unwillingness to admit need. The greatest battle many believers fight today is not with inefficiency, but with *super*efficiency. It's been bred into us by high-achieving parents, throughyears of high-pressure competition in school, and by that unyielding inner voice that keeps urging us to "Prove it to 'em! Show 'em you can do it without anyone's help!"

The result, painful though it is to admit, is a life-style of impatience. We become easily irritated—often angry. We work longer hours. Take less time off. Forget how to laugh. Cancel vacations. Allow longer and longer gaps between meaningful times in God's Word. Enjoy fewer and fewer moments in prayer and meditation. And all the while the specter of discouragement looms across our horizon like a dark storm front—threatening to choke out any remaining sunshine.

Say, my friend, it's time to declare it. You are not the Messiah of the twentieth century! There is no way you can keep pushing your life at that pace and expect to stay effective. Analyze yourself any way you please, you are H-U-M-A-N . . . nothing more. So? So slow down. So give yourself a break. So stop trying to cover all the bases and sell popcorn in the stands at the same time. So relax for a change!

Once you've put it in neutral, crack open your Bible to Exodus 18 and read aloud verses 18-27. It's the account of a visit Jethro made to the work place of his son-in-law. A fella by the name of Moses. Old Jethro frowned as he watched Moses flash from one need to another, from one person to another. From early morning until late at night the harried leader of the Israelites was neck-deep in decisions and activities. He must have looked very impressive—eating on the run, ripping from one end of camp to the other, planning appointments, meeting deadlines.

But Jethro wasn't impressed. "What is this thing that you are doing for the people?" he asked. Moses was somewhat defensive (most too-busy people are) as he attempted to justify his ridiculous schedule. Jethro didn't buy the story. Instead, he advised his son-in-law against trying to do everything alone. He reproved him with strong words:

> The thing that you are doing is not good. You will surely wear out. . . .

The Hebrew term means "to become old, exhausted." In three words, he told Moses to

CALL FOR HELP

The benefits of shifting and sharing the load? Read verses 22-23 for yourself. "It will be easier for you . . . you will be able to endure." That's interesting, isn't it? God wants our life-style to be easier than most of us realize. We seem to think it's more commendable and "spiritual" to hae that tired-blood, overworked-underpaid, I've-really-got-it-tough look. You know, the martyr complex. That strained expression that conveys "I'm working so hard for Jesus" to the public. Maybe *they're* fooled, but He isn't. The truth of the matter is quite the contrary. That hurried, harried appearance usually means, "I'm too stubborn to slow down" or "I'm too insecure to say 'no' " or "I'm too proud to ask for help."

Since when is a bleeding ulcer a sign of spirituality? Or no time-off and a seventy-hour week a mark of efficiency? When will we learn that efficiency is enhanced not by what we accomplish but more often by what we relinquish?

The world beginning to get you down? Feeling rotten? Too tired to pray . . . in too big a hurry? Ticked off at a lot of folks? Let me suggest one of the few four-letter words God loves to hear us shout when we're angry or discouraged:

HELP!

Deepening Your Roots

Exodus 18:13-27; Nehemiah 2:11-18; Philippians 2:19-30; Philippians 4:2-3

Branching Out

1. Ask someone to help you today.
2. Next time someone yells for help, immediately stop what you are doing and assist the person. Don't ask them what's wrong. Go help!
3. *Before* someone asks you to help . . . offer it.

Trophies

He was brilliant. Clearly a child prodigy . . . the pride of Salzburg . . . a performer *par excellence*.

At age five he wrote an advanced concerto for the harpsichord. Before he turned ten he had composed and published several violin sonatas and was playing from memory the best of Bach and Handel. Soon after his twelfth birthday he composed and conducted his own opera . . . and was awarded an honorary appointment as concertmaster with the Salzburg Symphony Orchestra. Before his brief life ended, he had written numerous operettas, cantatas, hymns, and oratorios, as well as forty-eight symphonies, forty-seven arias, duets, and quartets with orchestral accompaniment, and over a dozen operas. Some 600 works!

His official name was Johannes Chrysostomus Wolfgangus Amadeus Theophilus Mozart. With a handle like that, he *had* to be famous.

He was only thirty-five when he passed on. He was living in poverty and died in obscurity. His sick widow seemed indifferent to his burial. A few friends went as far as the church for his funeral but were deterred by a storm from going to the gravesite.

By the time anyone bothered to inquire, the location

of his grave was impossible to identify. The unmarked grave of Mozart—perhaps the most gifted composer of all time—became lost forever. No shrine marks his resting place for music lovers to visit. No granite-engraved etchings for admirers to read. No place for candles to burn, flowers to embellish, tourists to gather. Mozart has joined the immortal, eternal ages—forever absent from sight. He is gone.

Or is he? Unlike Caesar, the good he did lives after him. The evil is interred with his bones. Only a handful of music buffs could begin to list three or four evils of that Austrian-born artist. Then what good lives on? *His unique contributions*: his style, his eminent innovations, that "Mozart touch." No other sound is like it. It is his, altogether. *A timeless trophy*, created by his genius, captured on the score, bringing warmth and delight to endless generations. In his music, Mozart lives on. Unexcelled.

Several years ago one of my children and I walked through a cemetery. We paused and read the stones. We knew none of the deceased. It was a nostalgic, gripping encounter. Hand in hand we walked and talked. Softly. Thoughtfully. It was as though we were on sacred soil. Time stopped at each marker. Quietness swept over us as we drove away. I shall not soon forget what I learned.

First, *life is brief*. Terribly brief. On every stone there is a little dash . . . a horizontal line . . . illustrating time. Mozart's stone (wherever it is) reads:

1756-1791

That's it. But if only that "dash" could speak! It'd teach us the next lesson.

Second, *opportunity is now*. Not later. *Now*. Your contribution, small though it may seem, is unique and altogether yours. Whatever it may be—it becomes that timeless trophy you invest daily. The ancient aphorism I heard as a boy occasionally haunts me:

> Four things come not back: the
> spoken word, the sped arrow, time
> past, the neglected opportunity.

Third, *death is sure*. You can't dodge it, save by the Rapture. It's coming, friend. And at that time, like Mozart, you may seem insignificant to others. Forgotten, even. The only thing that will live on will be your personal contributions, your unique investments during your lifetime. Not your name . . . or your grave . . . but your timeless trophy.

Okay, so you're not brilliant, a prodigy, a composer of symphonies. What *are* you? A mother of two, three kiddos? An executive, a salesman, a retired military officer, a student, a nurse, a divorcee, minister, teacher, widow, farmer? Your trophy is *your contribution*—whatever and wherever. Known or unknown. It's your investment, your gifted "touch," that will live on far beyond the grave. God displays these trophies forever.

It is said of Abel:

> . . . God testifying about his gifts . . . though he is dead, he still speaks (Hebrews 11:4b).

Such trophies never tarnish.

Deepening Your Roots

Ruth 2:1-12; Titus 2:7-8; Hebrews 11:1-40

Branching Out

1. What would you like your epitaph to say?
2. What would you like to receive a trophy for? Are you working toward receiving it?
3. Encourage someone today who seems to feel insignificant. Comment on the importance of who they are to you and to others.

Fulfillment

Al Weidman polishes Porsche wheels. It's his bag. And (best of all) he *loves* it. How'd he get into it? Well, he got fed up with the rat race.

For fifteen years he worked for an internationally-known corporation. He was a number, not a person, to the firm. Became the purchasing agent with a swell salary . . . but that was it. He drove fifty-five miles to work every day to a building with no windows and a job with no fulfillment. Monotony turned into misery . . . discouragement led to dread as Al saw less and less to his family and more and more of the freeway.

He and Susan and their four kids began to pray:

> Lord, something *has* to happen! Do something, anything. Change our lives. This is no way to live. Lord, take over.

He did. Al got laid off.

Sounds weird, but it was one of the happiest days of his life. The squirrel cage finally ground to a halt. The fifteen-year addiction was, at last, broken by God Himself. Great! Only one problem—what now? Well, faith suddenly moved from back-burner theory to front-burner reality. Talk about cold-turkey! For the first time in their marriage, Al and Susan found themselves in the exciting spot of literally having to "trust in the Lord with all their hearts" rather than just memorize it in a Bible study group. The result? *Fantastic!* Through an amazing chain of events that nobody but the Lord could weave together, the man who once did purchasing for a corporation (hating every minute of it) now does polishing for dealerships all over Southern California . . . and points beyond.

He's having the time of his life. Never before has he experienced such depths of delight. Is he making a living? More than he dreamed possible—but keep in mind, that's no longer his motivation. When the Lord took Al and Susan through the experiential operating room, it was for radical surgery. Life did a flip-flop. They determined their priorities would no longer be sacrificed on the altar of temporal values. When God got through with that couple, His blessings came up in spades. The differences now? Well, for openers, he no longer feels trapped, crushed beneath the load of so-called essentials. *He's free*. Freed from a slavery that at times seemed as brutal and demanding as a nineteenth-century plantation owner. But there's one thing better than that. *He's fulfilled*. Satisfied. He's found his niche. The dread is gone. Each new dawn brings a fresh delivery of anticipation.

Fulfillment has to be one of life's choicest gifts. A major building block toward authentic happiness. Solomon must have had it in mind when he wrote in Proverbs 13:19:

> Desire realized is sweet to the soul. . . .

Who can measure up to the pleasure of that scene? The longing of the heart—unrevealed and deep—leads to *dreams*. These dreams float as time passes, refusing to be sunk by the anchors of hindrance and hardship. They grow into *possibilities* kept alive by hope and determination. Vague possibilities lead to concrete *opportunities* that stir up the soul with gratifying, satisfying stimulation . . . which ultimately becomes actual *accomplishment*, the ace trump of fulfillment. And that is sweet, writes David's wisest son.

I agree with Longfellow:

Tell me not, in mournful numbers,
  Life is but an empty dream!

. . . .

Lives of great men all remind us
  We can make our lives sublime,
And, departing, leave behind us
  Footprints on the sands of time.

Have you become a victim of routine? Beginning to think demoralizing thoughts like, "Aw, what's the use?" and, "It isn't worth the effort"? Starting to sigh rather than smile . . . focusing on the hurdles rather than the tape at the end of the race? If so, you have a lot of company. Surrendering to despair is man's favorite pastime. God offers a better plan, but it takes effort to grab it and faith to claim it. Like Oscar Hammerstein put it:

Climb every mountain, search high, and low,
  Follow every by-way, every path you know.

Climb every mountain, ford every stream,
Follow every rainbow, 'til you find your dream.[4]

Please—take it from one who, years ago, almost stopped climbing and searching and following—stay at it! Climbing and dreaming sure beat a stale life without windows . . . and a cage without release.

Deepening Your Roots

Joshua 14:6-12; Nehemiah 1:1-11; Nehemiah 2:1-5

Branching Out

1. What are you climbing toward? Is it really what you want? If not, why not do what Al and Susan did: pray.
2. Read the book: *With No Fear of Failure* if you need more encouragement or help in determining your "dream."
3. Write down three dreams you want to see happen to you in your lifetime. Start praying about these dreams and don't stop trusting God until all the "dreams" come true.

Procrastination

Allow me to introduce a professional thief.

Chances are you'd never pick this slick little guy out of a crowd, but many, over the years, have come to regard him as a formidable giant. Quick as a laser and silent as a moonbeam, he can pick any lock. Once inside, his winsome ways will captivate your attentions. You'll treat him like your best friend. But watch out. He'll strip you without a blink of remorse.

Master of clever logic that he is, the bandit will rearrange the facts just enough to gain your sympathies. When others call his character into question, you'll find yourself not only believing in him, but actually *quoting* and *defending* him. Too late, you'll see through his ruse and give him grudging credit as the shrewdest of all thieves. Some never come to such a realization at all. They stroll to their graves arm-in-arm with the very robber who has stolen away their lives.

His name? *Procrastination*. His specialty? Stealing time and incentive. Like the proverbial packrat, he makes off with priceless valuables, leaving cheap substitutes in their place: excuses, rationalizations, empty promises, embarrassment, and guilt. Like most crooks, this pro hits you when you're weak—the moment you relax your defenses. You wake up on a Saturday morning. It's been a beast of a week. Insistent voices of neglected tasks echo in your head and plead for attention. Suddenly your con-artist appears and begins to bargain with you. By sundown he's gone . . . and so is your day . . . and so is your hope.

You step on the bathroom scales and blink in disbelief. The dial tells you the truth—but the thief offers another interpretation. Stealing your surge of motivation, he whispers the magic word—*mañana*—and you reach for a donut to celebrate your philosophy:

> Never do today what you can put off 'til tomorrow.

You face a crucial decision this afternoon. It's been building up for two weeks. You've ignored it, dodged it, postponed it—but you must not do so any longer. Today is "D" day. You've talked yourself into it. Thirty minutes before the deadline, the thief offers the perfect alibi and back on the shelf goes your decision, growing another day larger.

No piper was better paid. No liar was better respected. No bandit better rewarded. No giant better treated.

You name it—he comes out a winner every time even though he's a hard-core outlaw. He can outtalk any student when it comes to homework. He can outthink any executive when it comes to correspondence. He can outwork any homemaker when it comes to vacuuming or doing dishes. He can outlast any parent when it comes to discipline. He can outsmart any salesman when it comes to selling. He has one basic product and he centers all his energy toward that single goal: defeat. By the sheer genius of suggestion he becomes the epitome of what he destroys: success.

There once lived a politician named Felix. He was a governor during the first century. Before him stood a prisoner named Paul. On two separate occasions, Felix listened to Paul tell his story, presenting in simple terms the matter of faith in Jesus Christ. Felix heard every word but passed off the message with similar comments:

> When Lysias the commander comes down, I will decide your case (Acts 24:22).
> Go away for the present, and when I find time, I will summon you (Acts 24:25).

The governor heard Paul, but he listened to the thief. He intentionally put off the most significant moment of his life—a decision he will never forget. Never. Why? Because he listened to the wrong counsel. It was only a subtle suggestion. It wasn't a bold-face lie, like "There is no heaven," or, "There is no hell." It was simply, "There is no *hurry*." Thereby the grim thief won another victory of defeat.

"How can *I* win?" you ask. What's the secret—the formula—for escaping this thief's intimidating web? How can I stop the giant from breaking and entering?

It's really very simple . . . so simple you won't believe it. All it takes is one word, perhaps the easiest word to utter in our language. Properly used, that single syllable carries more weight than a ton of good intentions. The thief cannot endure the sound of it. It sends him fleeing in frustration. If you use it often enough, he might get tired of hearing it—and start leaving you alone.

Curious? I'll make you a deal. I'll tell you the word if you'll promise to use it next time you're tempted to listen to the fast-talking embezzler. I have a warning, however. It may be easy—but it will require all the discipline you can muster to *mean*. To implement it will demand, in fact, the power of God Himself.

The word is "Now."

Deepening Your Roots

Proverbs 14:23; Proverbs 31:10-31; Ephesians 5:14-17

Branching Out

1. List two one-day projects you've put off doing. Choose one and get it done by tomorrow.
2. Don't take on any new project until you've completed those you've put off.
3. Write a letter today to someone you've been meaning to write to for months—maybe even years. Do it now.

Impacting Lives

In his book, *A Thinking Man's Guide to Pro Football*, Paul Zimmerman quotes a physicist who had made an incredible discovery. The man had the facts to prove that when a 240-pound lineman (capable of running 100 yards in eleven seconds) collides with a 240-pound running back (capable of covering the same distance in ten seconds), the resultant kinetic energy is "enough to move 66,000 pounds—or thirty-three tons—one inch."

That helps explain why some players stagger about the field mumbling to themselves after having their bell rung during a collision. the likelihood is that they have been hit on the helmet by a blow approaching 1,000 Gs. That means 1,000 times the force of gravity. Astronauts on takeoff experience approximately 10 Gs. Pilots tend to black out at about 20 Gs. A recent issue of *Sportsweek* magazine stated that "tests run on Detroit Lion's linebacker, Joe Schmidt, reportedly showed that he had to cope with blows which registered at 5,780 Gs." Small wonder that football, at various levels, kills twenty-eight players a year . . . or that half the veterans of pro ball will die before age fifty-eight . . . or that one survey revealed that each year thirty-two college and high school football players become paraplegics. The game has changed from merely a contact sport to a *collision* sport. With unbelievable force, athletes chosen for their abnormal size and remarkable speed, stun, cripple, and even kill each other upon impact.

That explains why Joe Namath admits that by the age of fifty he fully expects to have difficulty just putting one foot in front of the other . . . or why Merlin Olsen, scarcely forty years old, has severe, painful arthritis in both his knees. The human body was never designed by God to handle collisions of that magnitude, no matter how strong or coordinated or big it may be. We simply cannot take the physical impact.

What about spiritual impact? Well, that's a horse of a different wheelbase. It's doubtful that any impact, spiritually speaking, could ever be too great. In fact, the bigger the better. Most of us thrive on models that challenge our *status quo*, tough though they may be. It has always been so. Who can possibly gauge the impact an eighty-year-old Bedouin shepherd named Moses had on Egypt when he stood up against Pharaoh? Or how about Gideon when he successfully led that invasion with blown trumpets and broken pitchers and a stern battle cry? No one can measure the impact Elijah had on Ahab . . . or Nehemiah had on Tobiah . . . or Job had on Elihu . . . or John the Baptizer had on Israel . . . or Paul had on Agrippa . . . or Luther had on Rome . . . or Knox had on Bloody Mary . . . or all the God-appointed evangelists like Whitefield and Edwards and Wesley and Moody and Graham have had on England and America.

And how about *your* life? Who is it the Lord has used to model His message and challenge you to change, to shake off that tendency to settle for less than your full potential, to stretch and pursue and conquer new territory you once never dreamed possible? All of us can name at least one individual, can't we?

Here are four characteristics usually found in those who impact our lives:

1. *CONSISTENCY*. These folk are not restless flashes in the pan—here today, gone tomorrow. Neither are they given to fads and gimmicks. Those who impact lives stay at the task with reliable regularity. They seem unaffected by the fickle winds of change. They're *consistent*.

2. *AUTHENTICITY*. Probe all you wish, try all you like to find hypocritical flaws, and you search in vain. People who impact others are real to the core; no alloy covered over with a brittle layer of chrome, but solid, genuine stuff right down to the nubbies. They're *authentic*.

3. *UNSELFISHNESS*. Musn't forget this one! Hands down it's there every time. Those who impact us the most watch out for themselves the least. They notice our needs and reach out to help, honestly concerned about our welfare. Their least-used words are "I," "me," "my," and "mine." They're *unselfish*.

4. *TIRELESSNESS*. With relentless determination they spend themselves. They refuse to quit. Possessing an enormous amount of enthusiasm for their labor, they press on regardless of the odds . . . virtually unconcerned with the obstacles. Actually, they are like pioneers—resilient and rugged. They're *tireless*.

Who impacts lives? Who is it God uses to collide with

us so as to dent our frames and jolt our direction? The consistent, authentic, unselfish, tireless individuals who hate those words "let's just get by," and "it's too hard, let's just quit."

Chances are good that, without realizing it, you've been reading the profile of that single individual who has impacted your life more than any other person. And it's not some huge hulk who wore a helmet and shoulder pads, knocking people senseless. This person might even dislike football and wonder why in the world anybody would enjoy it.

Your mother. Don't forget to honor her on Mother's Day.

Deepening Your Roots

Exodus 1:15-22; Exodus 2:1-10; John 19:25-27

Branching Out

1. Besides sending your mother a card or flowers, write her a note and express to her something she has done for you in one of the four areas mentioned above. Be specific. Cite a certain time, place, statement, etc. She'll treasure this note.
2. Choose someone you could possibly care for or be a model to. Make it your prayer and effort in the next three months to work on this relationship.
3. Sacrifice. That's usually always part of being unselfish. Make a sacrifice today for someone else—but don't tell anyone you did so.
4. Adopt a mother. Find someone who can't be with her children today, or who is childless, and take her out to dinner. And if you're without a mother, adopt a substitute—maybe someone in a rest home, a widow in your church, etc.

Luxuries

Every morning as I drive to my office I pass a sight that leaves me drooling. I mash my nose against the glass and stare as long as I possibly can before checking back into reality. The object of my glare is a sleek, shiny boat that sits neatly backed into a driveway. Its fiberglass, shallow hull is deep blue, and it, along with its tailored trailer, is spotless. The wrap-around windshield is trimmed in dazzling chrome, the engine sparkles in the light of dawn, the accessories and special appointments reveal quality and class. Only one thing is missing—ME. The boat has the wrong owner! My imagination has taken me to Catalina and back . . . I've pulled my family and a dozen others on water skis . . . in fantasy I've waxed it and pampered it, tinkered with its details, and traveled the highways a hundred times with it close behind.

Now maybe your thing isn't something that floats. Well, take your pick. When it comes to luxuries, Southern California will spoil you—and I mean *fast*. Yours might be a pool out back . . . or lovely furnishings in the den . . . or a new suit rather frequently . . . or something with four on the floor and mag wheels . . . an ancient piece of sculpture . . . a mountain cabin . . . a trip to Rome . . . an Omega watch . . . an original oil painting by one of the masters . . . some expensive set of books . . . a hand-carved desk at your office . . . sophisticated sound equipment . . . an exquisite gem or some super-expensive antique. Swell, so much for dreaming.

You're probably thinking, like Plato wrote in *The Republic*,

WEALTH IS THE PARENT OF LUXURY . . .

and since you haven't got the cash, you're silly to think about spawning such "children" of wealth. Perhaps you're reluctant to entertain *any* dreams since daily reality turns them into nightmares of unfulfilled desire. It is possible that you are even laboring under the whip of that eternal taskmaster, Fear, who buffets your fondest fantasy with three brutal blows from his lash—public criticism, personal guilt, and perverted humility.

Why not meet your secret longing head-on? Why not declare that it's there in your thoughts, waiting for an honest, wise, and intelligent response? I have a most interesting time asking Christians what they would really like to have—what they'd enjoy owning. I've had them look around like somebody would squeal on them . . . or squirm like a worm, feeling uneasy as they admit that down deep inside they actually cherish some specific, luxurious wish. They occasionally whisper it to me under their breath as if confessing some vice or awful crime. Nonsense!

Whoever started the rumor that possessing something

expensive and luxurious was, in itself, suspect or sinful? Wasn't it Paul who openly declared that he had learned "how to enjoy prosperity . . . to be filled up . . . to have abundance . . ."? (Philippians 4:12, *Berleley*). He didn't spend all his days in overalls eating crackers and beans, drinking river water, and living under some bridge. Somehow, sometimes he lived with expensive luxuries . . . and admitted that such things were enjoyed to the fullest. You'll never convince me that Paul always looked grubby or was uneasy when surrounded by the elite.

Now the only wrong in all this is when expensive and luxurious things possess *us*. On that axis, everything shifts. When that happens, the green ghost of greed invades our dwelling and haunts our once-contented mind . . . like the farmer Jesus mentioned in Luke 12:16-21, who substituted the material for the spiritual. That man, said Jesus, was an outright fool. To him, luxuries were *essential* to life . . . they were his *sole means* of happiness and security. He became occupied with the gift and failed to consult with or recognize the Giver.

Do you have some hidden hope which might be labeled a luxury? Here's my advice:

1. Admit it . . . don't ignore it.
2. Evaluate it . . . don't fear it.
3. Plan for it . . . don't grab it.
4. Enjoy it . . . don't worship it.

And the next time you see a bright blue boat with a wrap-around windshield and a "For Sale" sign on it, admire it . . . but don't buy it. It might be the one that belongs behind my car.

Deepening Your Roots

Genesis 33:1-9; 2 Corinthians 8:1-15; Philippians 4:10-13

Branching Out

1. Write down a "dream" you'd like to come true.
2. Give away something that constantly possesses you—like a box of chocolates, or a gallon of ice cream, or some sports equipment. Do I dare mention your TV? Or let someone else use that boat or car for a weekend.

Holding Things Loosely

In her fine book, *Splinters in My Pride*, Marilee Zdenek reflects our deepest feelings. Those misty ones, hard to get a handle on. As the sights, sounds, and smells of different seasons began to create nostalgic itches inside me recently, she scratched one:

It was hard to let you go:
To watch womanhood reach out and snatch you
Long before the mothering was done.
But if God listened to mothers and gave in,
Would the time for turning loose of daughters ever come?

It was hard when you went away—
For how was I to know
The serendipity of letting go
Would be seeing you come home again
And meeting in a new way
Woman to woman—
Friend to friend.[5]

Letting go. Turning loose. Releasing the squeeze.

Being better at smothering than loving, we are blown away with the thought of relaxing our gargantuan grip. Because releasing introduces the terror of risk, the panic of losing control. The parting cannot happen without inward bleeding. The coward heart fears to surrender its prized toys. Even though it must say goodbye eventually.

Like releasing a dream; or allowing a child space to grow up; or letting a friend have the freedom to be and to do. What maturity that requires!

We are often hindered from giving up our treasures out of fear for their safety. But wait. Everything is safe which is committed to our God. In fact, nothing is really safe which is *not* so committed. No child. No job. No romance. No friend. No future. No dream.

Need some proof? Check out Abraham with his almost-adult son Isaac. Genesis 22. The old man's treasured delights rested in that boy. That relationship could well have bordered upon the perilous . . . if father would not come to grips with releasing son. But it was at that juncture that Jehovah-turned-pedagogue taught the patriarch a basic lesson in life.

> Take now your son, your only son, whom you love, Isaac, and go to the land of Moriah; and offer him there as a burnt offering . . . (Genesis 22:2).

It was time to turn him loose. Abraham might have started pleading or bargaining or manipulating, but that would not have caused the Almighty to choose an alternate course. No—Abraham had to open his hands and surrender on that ancient altar the one thing that eclipsed the Son from his heart. It hurt cruelly . . . beyond imagination. But it was effective.

The greater the possessiveness, the greater the pain.

The old miser within us will never lie down quietly and die obediently to our whisper. He must be torn out like a cypress tap root. He must be extracted in agony and blood like a tooth from the jaw. And we will need to steel ourselves against his piteous begging, recognizing it as echoes from the hollow chamber of self-pity, one of the most hideous sins of the human heart.

What is it God wants me to do? To hold things loosely, that He might reign without a rival. With no threats to His throne. And with just enough splinters in my pride to keep my hands empty and my heart warm.

Deepening Your Roots
Genesis 22:1-18; Philippians 3:7-21

Branching Out

1. Look around your house and name someone or something that would be hard to give up or let go of. Release your grip by telling God He can have the person or the object.
2. Take the time you normally spend watching your favorite TV show and spend the minutes instead with your spouse, a child, or a friend.
3. Buy a book you really want to read, and then give it away without reading it yourself.

Meditation

The lost art of the twentieth century is, in my opinion, meditation. We Americans are *masters* when it comes to activity . . . and entertainment . . . and planning . . . and preoccupation—but meditation? Forget it! Somehow we have the mistakeen idea that meditation demands hours and hours, that is the by-product of leisure (of which most of us have very little) and even laziness.

True meditation, however, is *not* daydreaming. It is *not* letting our minds drift here and there, thinking about nothing, and humming some religious melody with our eyes at half mast! Meditation is disciplined thought, forced on a single object or Scripture for a period of time. It is reflecting upon or pondering specific truths slowly, piece-by-piece . . . allowing our minds to dig deeply into a word, a phrase, an idea or principle from God's own Word. Meditation considers these things from every possible angle, with the purpose of getting insight, gaining practical benefit, and/or reaching some conclusion.

Meditation is not optional. The same Bible that commands us to "pray without ceasing," to "rejoice evermore," and "in everything give thanks" . . . also urges us to meditate. I find it interesting that this term appears no less than twenty times in the Word, with fourteen of those references occurring in the Psalms. In fact, the term only appears twice in all the New Testament—and in neither case is that the best translation. My point is this: meditation is essentially an Old Testament concept . . . and therefore understood from the viewpoint of its Hebrew origin.

Let me amplify. When you boil down the eighteen Old testament verses that mention "meditate" or "meditation," you discover that they come from one of two Hebrew words. The first is the term *HAG-GAH*, and the second, *SEE-AAGH*. Both these terms are frequently translated "talk," "speak," and "utter." They both convey the idea of "musing" and "pondering" and, surprising though it may seem, both are terms used for voicing a complaint, or moaning during suffering. They also convey the idea of imagination. Broad terms, aren't they?

Summing up these findings, I suggest that our meditation is to be broad enough to include imagination as we ponder God's Word, and in keepeing with the experiences and trials He brings our way. In other words, *we should link our lives with His Word* in our times of meditation.

Let me suggest five practical steps to follow in your development of this spiritual exercise. Let's use Proverbs 3:5-6 as our example:

1. Emphasize different words and phrases. In meditating on Proverbs 3:5-6, accent specific terms. "*Trust* in the Lord . . ." or "Trust in the Lord with *all* your heart." Think about *trusting* . . . and consider the vastness of that word *all*. When you read the warning ". . . do not lean on your *own* understanding," imagine the many ways you work things out for yourself.

2. *Paraphrase the verse. Make it personal.* Rethink and restate the verse using *your* words in the process. For example: "Lord, you are commanding me to turn my life over to you completely—to stop my habit of worrying and working things out my way, like I frequently do." Get the idea?

3. *Compare the verse with other Scripture.* Reflect on this in relation to two or three other passages. Weave them into your thoughts. How about Psalm 37:4-5 or Philippians 4:6-7 and 1 Peter 5:7? What an aid Scripture memory can be! It multiplies the value of meditation a hundredfold.

4. *Relate the verse to your present circumstance.* Let's suppose you are worried, you are restless and ill-at-ease within. You know it's wrong, but you can't seem to stop. You come across Proverbs 3:5-6, and decide to meditate on it. As you do, keep your problems in mind. Ask for insight from the Lord. List your worries one by one. Identify them. Look them over in the light of that passage. Tell Him your complaints as you meditate. Ask: "Am I ready to rely on God to take these things . . . or do I enjoy my worry?" Admit your weakness before Him.

5. *Use prayer as a follow-up.* Never fail to conclude with prayer. Ask Him to transfer your thoughts into your life. Thank Him in advance for the change He will bring.

"This book . . . shall not depart from your mouth, but

you shall meditate on it day and night, so that you may be careful to do according to all that is written in it . . ." (Joshua 1:8).

Deepening Your Roots

Joshua 1:6-8; Psalm 1:1-6; Psalm 119:97-104

Branching Out

1. List your worries. Now take point 4 above and do the steps I recommend.
2. Take five minutes of your lunch hour today and meditate on Proverbs 3:5-6.
3. Write out two verses you can meditate on this week.

Famine

The word hangs like an awful omen in our heads.

Mentally, we picture a brutal, grotesque image. Cow's hips protrude. Babies eyes are hollow. Bloated stomachs growl angrily. Skin stretches across faces tight as a trampoline. The outline of thee skull slowly emerges. Joints swell. Grim, despairing stares replace smiles. Hope is gone . . . life is reduced to a harsh existence as famine takes its toll. Those who have seen it cannot forget it. Those who haven't cannot imagine it.

We are told it is coming. "It's only a matter of time," declare the experts. There was a time when such predictions appeared only in science fiction books and novels, but no longer. Prophets of doom are now economists, university profs, and official spokesmen for our government, not to mention those authors who interpret our times as "threatening" or "terminal." Of greatest concern is the enormous population explosion that grips our globe. The statistics tell their own tale.

Our world reached the one billion mark by 1825. About one hundred years later we had doubled in population—*two* billion by 1925. By 1975 (only fifty years later) we doubled again—*four* billion. Should the trend continue we'll have *eight* billion by the year 2000 . . . and *sixteen* billion á short twelve years later, if by that long! The supply of food required to feed eight or more billion people is unbelievable. Worse than that, it's unattainable in light of our current agricultural systeme. The gaunt shells of humanity that now populate East Africa will some future day cast their shadows on North America, we're told. One reputable authority predicts that there will come a time when the world's big cities will be living on bacon bits, fruit in a tube, recycled foods,s protein pills and cakes, and reconstituted water.

For us who are so well fed, the idea of famine is foreign—almost a *fantasy*. It's something that plagues India or Biafra or China, never America! Fear of famine doesn't square with our "amber waves of grain," our "fruited plains," certainly not our streets lined with MacDonalds, thirty-one flavors, and innumerable shops bulging with every conceivable type of food.

My first rude awakening to the reality of hunger occurred early in 1958 when our troop ship full of U.S. Marines pulled into the harbor of Yokohama, Japan. We were so thrilled to see land, having been at sea for seventeen days, we were initially unaware of the barges full of Japanese men and women that encircled our ship. I later discovered that this was a common occurrence. They had come to paint the ship while we were at the dock for several days. Their pay in return? The garbage from our tables! The thought stunned me.

There is another kind of famine equally tragic . . . but far more subtle. God spoke of it through the prophet Amos. Listen to his words:

> "The time is surely coming," says the Lord God, "when I will send a famine on the land—not a famine of bread or water, but of hearing the words of the Lord. Men will wander everywhere from sea to sea, seeking the Word of the Lord, searching, running here and going there, but will not find it (Amos 8:11-13, TLB).

We may find physical famine almost impossible to believe, but how about a *spiritual* famine? You don't have to wait until the year 2000 for that! Take a trip across these United States. Or pick a country—*any* country. Talk about a famine! It's easy to misread the words of Amos. He didn't predict a lack of churches or chapels or temples or tabernacles or seminars or sermons. He spoke of "a famine . . . of hearing the words of the Lord." Remember, a famine does not mean an absence of something . . . but a *shortage* of it . . . a scarcity that creates a scene of starvation.

In our enlightened, progressive, modern age, an ancient, dusty prophecy is fulfilled. Hearing the unadulterated truth of God is a rare experience. How easy to forget that! We have come upon hard times when those who declare and hear the Word of God are a novelty.

How easy to be spoiled . . . presumptuous . . . sassy . . . ungrateful . . . when our spiritual stomachs are full! Funny thing—those who are full usually want *more*. We belch out increased demands rather than humble gratitude to God for our horn o'plenty.

Tell me, when was the last time you thanked God for the sheer privilege of hearing more of His Word than you could ever digest? And when did you last share just a crumb from your table?

That's why there's a famine.

Deepening Your Roots

Nehemiah 8:1-12; Mark 12:41-44; Acts 13:44-48

Branching Out

1. Write a relief agency this week and request information on how you can care for someone in need.
2. Now, do you see a famine for the Word of God close to your home? How can you relieve *that* desperate need—in your family . . . across the street . . . at your church?

Externals and Internals

Howard Snyder ticks me off.

He also makes me think. I agree, and I disagree. I laugh, and I sigh. Part of me wants to slug him yet two minutes later embrace him. I shake my head at his extreme generalizations . . . and shortly thereafter nod in amazement at his acute evaluations, accurate to the nth degree.

No man deserves all those emotions! But Snyder yanks them out of me as I read (for the third time) his 1976 controversial volume, *The Problem of Wine Skins*. Tough book. And don't let the title throw you. It has little to do with literal wine and even *less* with lather wineskins. But it has a lot to do with the principles behind Jesus' words in Luke 5:37-38.

> No one puts new wine into old wineskins, for the new wine bursts the old skins, ruining the skins and spilling the wine. New wine must be put into new wineskins (TLB).

Let that soak in. Obviously our Lord is distinguishing there between things that are essential (the wine) and things that are useful but not primary (the skins). Who needs wineskins if there is no wine? Wine, you see, represents the basics, the changeless, timeless, ever-potent, always-necessary message. The gospel. The Savior. The pristine truth of Scripture. And the wine-skins? Clearly, they represent that which is secondary, subsidiary, man-made. Stuff like structure, traditions (now don't stop reading), and patterns of doing things which have grown up around and encased the "wine." Got the picture?

The wineskins are the point of contact between the wine and the world. And as the surrounding pressure mounts from society, the skins tend to cease being flexible. They are seldom replaced. They get thicker, hard, less elastic . . . and ultimately unable to contain that volatile, vigorous vino within. They have reached the extreme inflexibility. And, unfortunately, few indeed are those who can tolerate fresh, new, supple bags to contain the wine. We much prefer the old—even if it's brittle and leaks—rather than the new.

That was the rub in Jesus' day. He was too radical and fresh in His approach. He irritated the old guard. Frowning, they kept asking questions like:

> Why do Your disciples transgress the tradition of the elders? For they do not wash their hands when they eat bread (Matthew 15:2).
>
> Why do you eat and drink with the tax-gatherers and sinners? (Luke 5:30).
>
> Why are they (*the disciples*) doing what is not lawful on the Sabbath? (Mark 2:24).

I mean, "Shame on you, Jesus! If you're going to expect our respect, keep your hands off our wineskins!"

You see, they confused the external container with

the internal treasure—even though the old Judaistic hand-me-downs were leaking badly.

Today we applaud His revolutionary determination. It was *that* quality which caused His contemporaries to mumble, "No man ever spoke as this Man does." But the barriers He scaled and the accusations He received increased the level of public anger to intense proportions. He wound up nailed to a cross, remember. And many returned to their old wineskins of religious tradition, thinking they were now safe from His words that had worried them for over three years.

But a remnant had tasted the wine. They had cultivated a new appetite. With new hearts they sang new songs. They preached a new hope from the new covenant. As new creations in Christ they offered "a new and living way" (Hebrews 10:20). Emerging from a cocoon of fear and intimidation, they flew free and bold. Willing to live in dens and caves of the earth, they swept the old world off its feet . . . "they turned it upside down," they literally "upset the world" (Acts 17:6).

That new breed of nontraditional thinkers emerged again in the sixteenth century. Unwilling to be crushed in the iron jaws of the papacy and all its trappings, they broke loose. Why? They despised traditional wineskins. They refused to clothe the resplendent riches of Christ in tacky religious rags. They chose to preserve the wine and replace the skins at the cost of being misunderstood. In their day they were quickly branded "heretics." Yet (strangely) today we extol them as courageous "reformers." It's amazing what a few hundred years will do to our perspective.

and what about *you*? Busy protecting and trying to preserve the wineskins? Working overtime carrying a torch of external tradition? Hey, I understand. I did that for almost twenty years of my Christian life. The wine got little of my attention as I patched up wineskins year after year. *What a waste!* Through a process of time and very painful events, I am breaking that nervous habit. The older I get, the less I care about the traditional skins and the more I crave the pure wine, the essentials, the external internals.

Thanks, Howard Snyder. I needed the reminder. But you still tick me off!

Deepening Your Roots
Luke 5:36-39; Galatians 2:6

Branching Out

1. Evaluate yourself and see if you can spot some traditionalism in your thinking or actions. If so, get bold and sever the old wineskin of traditionalism from your life.
2. Find a copy of Snyder's book at your local Christian bookstore. Allow him to challenge your thinking.

Simplicity

The scene was thick. The clouds were heavy and dark gray. The mood was tense. It was no time to take a walk in the park or stroll down Pennsylvania Avenue. The smell of death was in the air. A decision was essential. With paper and pen in hand, the lean, lank frame of a lonely man sat quietly at his desk. The dispatch he wrote was sent immediately. It shaped the destiny of a nation at war with itself.

It was a simple message . . . a style altogether his. No ribbons of rhetoric were woven through the note. No satin frills, no enigmatic eloquence. It was plain, direct, brief, to the point. A bearded Army officer soon read it with a frown. It said:

> April 7, 1865, 11 A.M.
>
> Lieut. Gen. Grant,
>
> Gen. Sheridan says, "If the thing is pressed, I think that Lee will surrender."
>
> Let the thing be pressed.
>
> A. Lincoln

Grant smiled in agreement. He did as he was ordered. Exactly two days later at Appomattox Court House,

General Robert E. Lee surrendered. "The thing was pressed" and the war was ended.

SIMPLICITY. Profound, exacting, rare simplicity. Lincoln was a master of it. His words live on because of it. When assaulted by merciless critics, many expected a lengthy, complex defense of his actions. It never occurred. When questioned about his feelings, he answered, "I'm used to it." When asked if the end of the war or some governmental rehabilitation program might be the answer to America's needs, he admitted quite simply, "Human nature will not change." In response to a letter demanding the dismissal of the Postmaster General, he wrote, "Truth is generally the best vindication against slander." When encouraged to alter his convictions and push through a piece of defeated legislation by giving it another title, he reacted with typical simplicity, "If you call a tail a leg, how many legs has a dog? Five? No, calling a tail a leg don't *make* it a leg!"

SIMPLICITY. The difference between something being elegant or elaborate. The difference between class and common. Between just enough and too much. Between concentrated and diluted. Between communication and confusion.

Between:

Hence from my sight—nor let me thus pollute mine eyes
with looking on a wretch like thee, thou cause of my ills;
I sicken at thy loathesome presence . . .

and:

Scram!

SIMPLICITY. *Economy* of words mixed with *quality* of thought held together by *subtlety* of expression. Practicing a hard-to-define restraint so that some things are left for the listener or reader to conclude on his own. Clear and precise . . . yet not overdrawn. Charles Jehlinger, a former director of the American Academy of Dramatic Arts, used to instruct all apprentice actors with five words of advice:

Mean more than you say.

It has been my observation that we Christians say all . . . too much, in fact. Instead of stopping with a concise statement of the forest—explicit and simple—we feel compelled to analyze, philosophize, scrutinize, and moralize over each individual tree . . . leaving the other person weary, unchallenged, confused, and (worst of all!) *bored*. Zealous to be ultra-accurate, we unload so much trivia the other person loses the thread of thought, not to mention his patience. Bewildered, he wades through the jungle of needless details, having lost his way, as well as his interest. Instead of being excited over the challenge to explore things on his own, lured by the anticipation of discovery, he gulps for air in the undertow caused by our endless waves of verbiage.

The longer I study Jesus' method of communicating, the more convinced I become that His genius rested in His ability to simplify and clarify issues that others confused and complicated. He used words anyone could understand . . . not just the initiated. He said just enough to inspire and motivate others to think on their own, to be inquisitive, to search further. And He punctuated his teaching with familiar, earthy, even humorous illustrations that riveted mental handles to abstract truths. Best of all . . . He didn't try to impress people. All these things led others to seek His counsel and thrive on His instruction.

If He could summarize my thoughts for me today, I believe He would offer this advice:

- Make it clear.
  - Make it simple.
    - Emphasize the essentials.
      - Forget about impressing.
        - Leave some things unsaid.

We've got the greatest message on earth to declare. Most people have either never heard it or they've been confused because someone has complicated the issues. Jesus says, "If the thing is simplified, they will surrender."

Let the thing be simplified.

Deepening Your Roots

Job 16:3; Job 18:2, John 21:4-14

Branching Out

1. Check your speech. Do you use big words around people who do not have a large vocabulary? Work at speaking on their level.
2. Don't speak for five minutes today when around a group. How did you feel during those five minutes?

Keeping Your Word

March 11, 1942, was a dark, desperate day at Corregidor. The Pacific theater of war was threatening and bleak. One island after another had been buffeted into submission. The enemy was now marching into the Philippines as confident and methodical as the star band in the Rose Bowl parade. Surrender was inevitable. The brilliant and bold soldier, Douglas MacArthur, had only three words for his comrades as he stepped into the escape boat destined for Australia:

I SHALL RETURN.

Upon arriving nine days later in the port of Adelaide, the sixty-two-year-old military statesman closed his remarks with this sentence:

I CAME THROUGH AND I SHALL RETURN.

A little over 2½ years later—October 20, 1944, to be exact—he stood once again on Philippine soil after landing safely at Leyte Island. This is what he said:

> This is the voice of freedom. General MacArthur speaking. People of the Philippines: I HAVE RETURNED!

MacArthur kept his word. His word was as good as

his bond. Regardless of the odds against him, including the pressures and power of enemy strategy, he was bound and determined to make his promise good.

This rare breed of man is almost extinct. Whether an executive or an apprentice, a student or a teacher, a blue or white collar worker, a Christian or a pagan—rare indeed are those who keep their word. The prevalence of the problem has caused the coining of terms painfully familiar to us in our era: *credibility gap*. To say that something is "credible" is to say it is "capable of being believed, trustworthy." To refer to a "gap" in such suggests a "breach or a reasoned for doubt."

Jurors often have reason to doubt the testimony of a witness on the stand. Parents, likewise, have reason at times to doubt their children's word (and vice versa). Citizens frequently doubt the promises of politicians, and the credibility of an employee's word is questioned by the employer. Creditors can no longer believe a debtor's verbal promise to pay and many a mate has ample reason to doubt the word of his or her partner. This is a terrible dilemma! Precious few do what they *say* they will do without a reminder, a warning, or a threat. Unfortunately, this is true even among Christians.

Listen to what the Scriptures have to say about keeping your word:

> Therefore each of you must put off falsehood and speak truthfully to his neighbor . . . (Ephesians 4:25 NIV).

> And whatever you do, whether in word or deed, do it all in the name of the Lord Jesus . . . (Colossians 3:17 NIV).

> O LORD, who may abide in Thy tent?
> Who may dwell on Thy holy hill?
> He who walks with integrity . . .
> And speaks truth in his heart (Psalm 15:1-2).

> It is better not to vow than to make a vow and not fulfill it (Ecclesiastes 5:5 NIV).

> When a man . . . takes an oath to obligate himself by a pledge, he must not break his word but must do everything he said (Numbers 30:2 NIV).

Question: Judging yourself on this matter of keeping your word, are you bridging or widening the credibility gap? Are you encouraging or discouraging others? Let me help you answer that by using four familiar situations.

1. When you reply, "Yes, I'll pray for you"—do you?
2. When you tell someone they can depend on you to help them out—can they?
3. When you say you'll be there at such-and-such a time—are you?
4. When you obligate yourself to pay a debt on time—do you?

Granted, no one's perfect. But if you fail, do you own up to it? Do you quickly admit your failure to the person you promised and refuse to rationalize around it? If you do, you are *really* rare . . . but a person of genuine integrity. And one who is an encouragement and can encourage others.

Do you know something? I know another One who promised He would return. He, too, will keep His word. In fact, He's *never* broken one promise. There's no credibility gap with Him.

He will return!

Deepening Your Roots

1 Chronicles 17:16; 2 Chronicles 16:12-15; Psalm 145-13

Branching Out

1. What's a promise you made someone but have failed to keep? Go back and keep that promise this week, or let the person know the time and date you expect to fill that unfulfilled promise.
2. Make a promise to someone today . . . and fulfill it.
3. Find a promise in Scripture and write it down. Claim it for yourself. Encourage yourself.

Surprises

The feelings are familiar. Mouth open. Eyes like saucers. Chill up the spine. Heart pounding in the throat. Momentary disbelief. We frown and attempt to piece the story together without a script or narrator. Sometimes alone, occasionally with others . . . then *boom!* "The flash of a mighty surprise" boggles the mind, leaving us somewhere between stunned and dumb with wonder. "Am I dreaming or is a miracle happening?" So it is with surprises.

O. Henry did it with his endings. World War II, with its beginning. Surprises start parties and they stop partnerships. They solve murders, they enhance birthdays and anniversaries, they embellish friendships. Kids at Christmas love 'em. Parents expect 'em. Coaches use 'em. Politicians diffuse 'em.

We like 'em and we hate 'em. Just a few one-liners illustrate both reactions.

> "Dr. Brown would like to discuss your X-rays right away."
>
> "Class, take out a clean piece of paper . . . it's pop quiz time."
>
> "We've been on the wrong road for an hour. Here, look at the map."

"The alarm didn't go off. It's almost noon!"

"Hello . . . I'm calling from the bank regarding your checking account."

"Honey, the doctor heard *three* heartbeats today."

"The boss wants to see you. No need to take off your coat."

"Congratulations—you made the cheerleading squad."

"We are happy to inform you your manuscript has been accepted for publication."

"This is Officer Franklin. We have your son down at the station.He's under arrest."

"The tumor we suspected to be malignant is actually benign."

"It isn't a carburetor problem, ma'am. Your whole engine is shot!"

"Sweetie, that wasn't leftover stew. It was Alpo."

"Did you know the bathroom scales weigh twelve pounds *light*?"

"Mom . . . Dad . . . Byron wants to marry me!"

And on and on they go. The highs and lows of our lives are usually triggered by surprises. Within split seconds we are sobbing or laughing like crazy . . . staring in bewildered confusion or wishing we would wake up from a dream.

Ever stopped to trace the surprises through the Bible? That Book is *full* of them when you look at certain events through the eyes of people in that day. Like . . . when Adam and Eve stumbled upon Abel's fresh grave. When Enoch's footprints stopped abruptly. When Noah's neighbors first realized it was sprinkling. When aged Sarah said, *"Ze angel vasn't kidding, Abe!"* When Moses' ears heard words from a bush that wouldn't stop burning. When Pharaoh's wife screamed, *"He's dead! Our son is dead!"* When manna first fell from the sky. When water first ran from the rock. When Jericho's walls came tumbling down. When a ruddy runt named David whipped a rugged warrior named Goliath. When a judge named Samson said yes instead of no. When a prophet named Jonah said no instead of yes. When a woman from Samaria had a Jewish Stranger tell her all her secrets. When the disciples discovered that Judas was guilty. When the only perfect One who ever lived was nailed to a criminal's cross. When Mary saw Him through the fog that epochal Sunday morn.

And that's just a quick review of the snapshots. I mean, if we had time to enjoy the whole album, we'd be up 'til midnight. It's gasp-and-gulp city right up to the end.

And speaking of the end, that last page will be the *greatest* shock of all. Talk about "the flash of a mighty surprise!" How does "like a thief in the middle of the night" grab you? How about "in a moment . . . in the twinkling of an eye?" Gives me the willies just *writing* those words. Imagine all those open mouths, eyes like saucers, spine-tingling chills high up in the clouds!

Jesus' return will be the absolute greatest surprise. Well, maybe I had better not say *that*. The *greatest* surprise is that people like us will be included in the group, stunned and dumb with wonder. Let's face it, that won't be just a surprise or a dream. That'll be a flat-out miracle.

Deepening Your Roots

Genesis 17:15-17; Genesis 18:9-14; Joshua 6:1-22; 1 Corinthians 15:52-58

Branching Out

1. Plan and throw a surprise party for someone. Or kidnap a friend early Saturday morning and take him out for breakfast.
2. Ask God to surprise you in some creative way this week.

Growing Strong

Here's a surprise for you: Summer is here. Oh, I know it's not officially that season until June 21 . . . but I'm eager for some days of rest and relaxation. I suspect you are, too. So, on to summer.

Conclusion

Some verses from the Bible make us smile. We have enjoyed them together as we considered a few such verses through the pages of this book. Some references are penetrating and convicting as they cause us to look into the mirror of truth and face facts. We've considered a number of those, too. Others are comforting, giving us hope to go on, regardless. A few introduce us to brand new scenes we'd never seen before. Maybe that has happened as you've worked your way through these pages.

There is one verse, however, that never fails to take us by the shoulders and shake us awake. It comes to my mind because it draws upon a word picture of seasons to make its point. You may recall reading it before.

> "Harvest is past, summer is ended,
> And we are not saved" (Jeremiah 8:20).

Does that describe *you*? If so, may I suggest that you come to terms with this need. Seasons follow a cycle: winter, spring, summer, autumn . . . so that the earth might enjoy all the things its Creator designed for it to enjoy.

Your life is, in many ways, the same. Multiple seasons, not a long, monotonous marathon of pointless futility; but variety, peaks and valleys, change and color. How tragic to move through the seasons without realizing their ultimate purpose! And that is that?

Go back to the verse. Read it aloud. The purpose is obvious: that we might *be saved* . . . that we might not trust in ourselves but in Jesus Christ, our Creator Lord . . . and, in doing so, receive from Him the assurance of abundant life now and eternal life forever.

Throughout this book I've been truthful with you. Now it's your turn to be truthful with yourself. Are you absolutely certain that you possess His gifts of forgiveness and purpose? You can have that assurance if your traveling Companion through the year is the Son of God. He alone can give meaning to the cycle as He enables you to grow strong in all the seasons of your life.

FOOTNOTES

1. Sir William Osler, *Familiar Quotations*, ed. John Bartlett (Boston: Little, Brown and Company, 1955), p. 744b.
2. Henry W. Baker, ''Art Thou Weary, Art Thou Languid?''
3. Walter Martin, *Screwtape Writes Again* (Santa Ana, California: Vision House Publishers, 1975), p. 16.
4. Richard Rogers and Oscar Hammerstein, ''Climb Every Mountain,'' 1959.
5. Marilee Zdenek, *Splinters in My Pride*, Part I (Waco, Texas: Word Books, 1979). [n.p.].